THE END OF THE RELIGIOUS LIFE

THE END OF THE RELIGIOUS LIFE

Robert Faricy, S.J.

WINSTON PRESS

Cover photograph: Cyril A. Reilly

Cover design: Tom Egerman

Scripture quotations marked RSV are from the *Revised Standard Version Common Bible*, copyright © 1973 by the Division of Christian Education of the National Council of the Churches of Christ in the U.S.A. Used by permission.

Scripture quotations marked JB are from *The Jerusalem Bible*, copyright © 1966 by Darton, Longman & Todd, Ltd. and Doubleday & Company, Inc. Used by permission of the publisher.

Scripture quotations marked RF are translations or paraphrases by the author.

Library of Congress Catalog Card Number: 82-50709

ISBN: 0-86683-690-X

Printed in the United States of America.

5 4 3 2 1

Winston Press, Inc.
430 Oak Grove
Minneapolis, Minnesota 55403

To the Very Reverend Pedro Arrupe, S.J.,
with great love and admiration

"Behold, I make all things new." (Rev. 21:5 RSV)

ACKNOWLEDGMENTS

Many persons have helped me to write, to rewrite, and to order the material in this book. In particular, I want to thank Sister Lucy Rooney, S.N.D.de N., Fathers Francis A. Sullivan, S.J., and John Navone, S.J., and several people at Winston Press, especially John Welshons, Florence Flugaur, Jan Johnson, Dee Ready, and Hermann Weinlick. I am grateful to all of them for their encouraging help and their patience.

CONTENTS

THE END OF THE RELIGIOUS LIFE

This book is for priests, sisters, and brothers who belong to religious orders and congregations. I hope that you will read it listening to the Lord, open to what God will say in your heart through the words in this book and beyond them.

This book is written for a time of discouragement and loss of hope in the religious life, for the present age which is witnessing the apparent end of the religious life.

Not only are whole provinces dying out, but entire orders and congregations are moribund. Some, of course, will be renewed and will survive. But many will not. They have nearly come to the end. They are in their last generation, terminal cases.

The question of the renewal of the religious life is a life-or-death question. We are in a time of transition, and many groups will not survive the transition. Some orders and congregations will become revitalized, truly refounded. For those that do not, it is the end of the line.

Change, as we now know so well, is not enough to bring about renewal. Necessary, yes; but not sufficient.

Only the Lord, in the power of his Holy Spirit, can give the religious life the new life it needs for renewal.

The title, *The End of the Religious Life,* is deliberately ambiguous: *End* can mean "the finish," "the terminal point," "death." *End* can also mean "purpose" or "goal." The title is a pun. Its significance is this: Only to the extent that the religious life recovers anew its purpose and begins anew to live toward its goal will it survive. That purpose, that goal, is holiness. And holiness is a question of God's grace, of his Spirit being poured into our hearts. Only the sanctifying Spirit can sanctify, make holy.

Only the Holy Spirit can renew the religious life.

A rich and powerful man gave a banquet and sent his

secretary to invite many people. But they declined his invitation, sending him their various excuses. The man's secretary reported to him all the turned-down invitations with the excuses; the rich man was furious. He told his secretary, "Go out into the city streets and round up the marginal people— the poor, the lame, the blind—and bring them to my banquet" (Lk. 14:16-21 RF).

This book might be considered an invitation to religious to come to the Lord's banquet, the banquet of renewal in his Holy Spirit. But the book is not addressed to those religious who are well off; they would not accept the invitation. It is, rather, for those religious who are—and who know they are—like the author, poor, lame, blind.

Come to the banquet.

Chapter One

THE CHARISM OF THE INSTITUTE

Some Impressions of Change

The guidebooks to Rome encourage the tourist to visit the Church of the Holy Cross in the heart of the city. The rich baroque interior is worth seeing, and—in the words of one guidebook—"two nuns in blue and white habits kneel reverently before the altar." If you go there, however, you will find the church closed. Or, should you find it open at an odd moment of the day, you will not find the two nuns.

The convent associated with the church, the generalate of a congregation of sisters, can no longer supply sisters to kneel in front of the altar. Perpetual adoration has been discontinued because most of the sisters in the convent are too busy. The church is open sometimes for Mass at mid-day, and for vespers, but even if you go at those times you will not see the sisters as described in the tourist guidebooks—in long blue and white habits with veils. The habits are of various hues and lengths, and several of the sisters no longer wear veils. Some changes have taken place.

More startling are the changes in the life of my friend Grace. Grace recently received her doctorate in biblical theology from the Pontifical Gregorian University. She knows more theology and sacred Scripture, to say nothing of biblical languages, than the vast majority of priests. Grace wears earrings two inches in diameter; her hair is stylishly cut; she dresses not expensively but in excellent taste. Grace is an American Sister of Mercy. Meeting her, you might not guess that she is a nun, completely dedicated to God and to serving him as a sister.

In my own community at the Gregorian University, the lifestyle of the Jesuit professors and others who make up the community no longer has the uniformity and regular schedule it had twenty years ago. Then, the Jesuits all wore cassocks, rose at the same time, went to bed at the same time, and rarely went out of the house or spent more than four dollars a month.

Today, Jesuits at the Gregorian University all dress differently, no two alike. Each keeps his own schedule. At almost every meal, several are missing, dining outside the community.

Some changes, then, have taken place in the religious life, in the lives of the men and women who belong to religious orders and congregations. I am not referring to the exceptions—to the religious priests in Latin America who move by night with the guerrilla patrols, to the American priests and sisters who have formed their own organization for homosexual religious men and lesbian religious women, to the sisters who are mayors or firemen, to the priests and brothers and sisters who have died as martyrs because they denounced grave social injustices or acted to remedy them. I am referring to the average religious, and to the changes in his or her everyday life.

What one wears on one's body and at what time one gets up in the morning are not, of course, essentials. A community is not religious or even a community because its members all dress alike, rise at the same time in the morning, and retire at the same hour at night. Externals do not make the monk.

And yet, external changes tell us something. They indicate changes going on inside at a deeper level. Just what is taking place at the deeper level? What is going on today in the religious life?

The seismographs are jumping wildly. Large masses are moving under the surface. What masses? How are they moving? Where are they going? And what might we expect to happen next?

This book contains some reflections that might help us as religious to think more clearly about the religious life today and to understand it better. The aim of these reflections, then, is not to make any moral value judgments, but to try to understand the changes and apparent upheavals in the religious life today.

Why have there been so many changes in religious orders of men and women? Why are there so few religious vocations? Is the religious life dying out? In 2050 will there still be Jesuits and Dominicans and Sisters of the Holy Child? What is happening today in the religious life is closely connected with what is called "the charism of the institute."

Every religious institute has its own charism, its own special grace. More exactly, each religious congregation and order has its own particular cluster of charisms, its own unique way of walking in the Spirit of loving consecration and service. By common usage, this special group of charisms that each institute has from God is called the charism of the institute.

What Is "the Charism of the Institute"?
Sometimes it is called "the charism of the founder"—because often the graces offered to the order or congregation are those found in a primordial kind of way in the life of the institute's founder. However, the charism of the institute can be more or less than, or simply different from, the graces of the founder's life. Furthermore, the life of the founder may not offer even a good example: I know of one foundress who died outside the congregation and outside the Church. True, every Franciscan institute shares in the spirit of Francis of Assisi, but the Capuchins do so in one way, the Friars Minor in another, and each Franciscan institute in its own particular way. Every Dominican institute will have in some way the charism of Dominic, but each in its own way: A cloistered contemplative Dominican institute will not try to live the Dominican charism in the same way as will teaching Dominicans.

The Second Vatican Council in its decree on *The Appropriate Renewal of the Religious Life* has underlined the importance of the charism of the institute. The "fundamental norm" and the "supreme law" of every religious institute always remains "the following of Christ as proposed by the gospel" (section 2). This fundamental norm and supreme law is also a fundamental and supreme grace: to leave all things and, following Jesus in consecrated celibacy, to live with him in obedience to the Father even unto death. It is the basic charism of the religious life. This fundamental and supreme charism of the religious vocation, like a beam of light hitting a diamond and refracted through the diamond's different facets, takes a different form in each religious institute. Not, then, that each religious congregation or order has a completely different charism; each has a unique form of the one common fundamental and supreme charism of following Jesus in the religious life.

No formula can adequately express the charism of a religious institute. A charism can be appreciated, grasped, made somehow perceptible only as we see it expressed in people who have that charism. The charism of a congregation or an order is grace; and grace is personal relationship with the Lord—in his power and love. Charisms exist in persons, not really in words, books, or documents. For example, the Jesuit charism can be briefly described as a cluster of graces: contemplation in action, apostolic mobility, Jesuit humility and poverty, the spirit of Ignatius Loyola's *Spiritual Exercises,* Jesuit obedience, loyalty to the pope, and so on. But such a description does not do justice to the reality of the charism as lived.

A charism is a particular grace, given to some but not to all, for the benefit of others and as a special way of relating to the Lord. The charism of an institute, then, is the particular grace given—or at least offered—to the members of that institute, as an apostolic gift (including the apostolate of prayer) and as a special way to be in relationship with the Lord (in prayer and in other activities). The point is that the institute's unique charism is a grace given to individuals.

An inadequate theology might distinguish "charism as mission" and "charism as grace"; the former would apply collectively to the whole congregation, and the latter to individual persons. But a charism is precisely a grace-for-mission; the two aspects cannot be separated. And the charism of an institute is given to an order or a congregation *only insofar* as it is given to individual persons. Conversely, the persons have a certain claim on that charism, a certain "right" to that grace by reason of belonging to the particular institute.

How Can the Charism of the Institute Be Renewed?
Two questions arise: (1) how can the charism of my institute be renewed in my whole community?; and (2) how can it be renewed in me?

The material on "the charism of the institute" or "the charism of the founder" that has appeared in article and book form since the Council enlightens me considerably as to what in general the "charism of the institute" *is*. And it tells me to some extent how to find out about the charism of my own religious institute so that I can better understand what it is.

But the authors do not tell me *how to obtain it*; they do not enlighten me as to *how to get a greater abundance of my institute's charism*. Any religious can leave a deep theological knowledge of his or her institute's charism to the experts, to those who have the training and the apostolate to investigate such matters. But the obtaining and renewing of the charism cannot be left to others.

I am called to have the particular charism of my institute. I have a right to a fullness of that charism. And I want my whole order or congregation to be renewed in its charism. I want to be more what the Lord calls me to be. And I want my whole community to be more what the Lord calls it to be.

How can the charism of the institute be renewed? "The ✓ appropriate renewal of the religious life," Vatican II's document on the subject tells us, "involves two simultaneous processes: (1) a continuous return to the sources of all Christian life and to the original inspiration behind a given institute and (2) an adjustment of the institute to the changed conditions of the times" (section 2). These two movements—the "continuous return" to the gospel and to the institute's origins, and the "adjustment" to contemporary conditions—form the double dynamic of the renewal of the charism of the institute. That is, the renewal of the institute's particular charism consists in somehow recovering the gospel charism of following Jesus according to the counsels, in the shape it took in the beginnings of the institute, and—moreover—in recovering it in a way ✓ suitable to today's problems and opportunities.

But the question remains: How can we do that? We can study New Testament exegesis regarding the gospel roots of the religious life. We can study the lives and the letters and the documents of our founders. We can investigate historically the first generations of our institutes. We can form research and study committees, and discuss. These things have been done, and continue to be done. They are good things. But they have not renewed the charism of any institute. Nor can they.

We know the limitations of these efforts. First, no one can define with any exactness the charism of an institute; charisms possess a transcendent quality that escapes definition. They are graces from the Lord. They are mysteries. As with any real mystery, I can know more and more about a charism, but I can never fully understand it.

Secondly, having the charism is far more important than describing it. And describing the charism presents insuperable difficulties when I cannot find it anywhere fully alive. If I myself do not have the charism in any fullness, how can I understand it? If my order or my congregation lives its unique charism only weakly, or wrongly, or formalistically, trying to get by pretty much just on a natural level, how can I find the needle that is my institute's charism in a haystack of busy-ness surrounded by a dense fog of discouragement or—worse—of euphoric complacency that "we are renewed"?

So what can we do? Two things. First, we can recognize the need for the renewal of the charism of our own particular institute—in the whole community and in each one of us. Secondly, since we are dealing with grace, and since the way to get grace or to have it in greater abundance is to ask the Lord for it, we can pray—for ourselves and for our institutes—that the Lord renew us in the charisms of our religious orders and congregations.

The Evolution of the Religious Life of the Institute

Why the need? What has happened in the religious life that calls for a renewal of community charisms, of the charisms proper to the various religious institutes? Why does my generation of Jesuits, for example, seem to lack the apostolic and contemplative power of Ignatius Loyola and his companions? Where are today's Francis Xaviers with the Jesuit charism of mission? Where are our Peter Fabers with divinely inspired discernment of spirits? Where are our contemplatives like Ignatius? And where has the power in our prayer and in our apostolate gone?

Martyrdom, surely, is a charism and a charismatic manifestation; and we do have martyrs, more than ever before. But where are—in *power*—the other gifts that made up what we call "the Jesuit charism"? Where are the contemplation in action, the Jesuit poverty, the third degree of humility, the familiarity with God, the tears?

I do not at all accept the thesis that outstanding charisms are only for the first generation or the first few generations of an institute. If that were true, then most of us have made serious mistakes in joining established communities; we should get out and join a community that is still in its first generation. This thesis is just a rationalization of the status quo, an intellectually dishonest justification of the fact that we are not like the first generations. We should be like them. We are called to be like them.

If the Second Vatican Council and the Charismatic Renewal and the many, many martyrs today tell us anything, they tell us that outstanding charisms are for now. The same stands true for the religious life and for every religious institute.

But Francis and Dominic and Ignatius were saints. Angela Merici and Julie Billiart and Mother Seton were saints. We, too, are called to be saints. The only failure I can have is not to be a saint.

So there is no excuse. Our religious orders and congregations are called to move in the power of the Spirit of Jesus and according to the original charisms proper to our religious congregations and orders.

What has gone wrong? Why have the charisms proper to our institutes diminished so greatly? Why have they nearly died out? It would take more learning, not to say more space, than I have here to do a pathology and to enumerate causes of the moribund condition of our community charisms.

Briefly, in the evolution of the religious life, the "letter" was gradually substituted for the "spirit." The original charism of the early generations was put into normative guidelines and rules so that the charism could be communicated and explained to succeeding members of the community. The purpose was to explain and to help. But the explanations gradually hardened into rules of external conduct; required interior attitudes became narrowly defined and legislated; and normative and even legalistic edifices grew up slowly in place of the original grace. The letter always tends to replace the spirit.

Then, with the renewal of the institutional structures of religious communities after the Second Vatican Council, much of this rigidity disappeared; innovation and flexibility became more prevalent; the "letter" faded. But the Spirit has not yet fully taken its place. Within the framework of renewed structures of the religious life, we seem to have words, formulae, and even elaborate plans. We have studies: sociological, psychological, financial. And we have documents: from chapters, from councils, from committees. But we do not yet see the powerful charisms that were at work in the beginnings of religious communities.

Following cultural anthropologist Victor Turner—see *Image and Pilgrimage in Christian Culture* (New York: Columbia University Press, 1978), p. 252—we can identify three successive phases of evolution regarding the charism of an institute. We can call the community's first few generations the "spontaneous phase." This phase includes the institute's foundation and rapid numerical expansion. This early period is characterized by freedom in sharing the things of the Spirit, by flexibility and spontaneity, by the exciting sense of creating together something new from God. The charism of the institute is manifested in powerful gifts of prayer and of apostolate. New works are established. People are healed. Evil spirits are cast out. Great numbers are converted.

Gradually, the expansion slows and begins to level off. The situation stabilizes. We can call this stable period the "normative phase." The original spirit of the community has flagged. The power has disappeared. Norms are established in an effort to hang on to the spirit and the unity that the force of the institute's charism formerly created.

Eventually, the norms cease to function, and we enter the third phase. The norms become outmoded and begin to be discarded. The community begins to lose its sense of identity and its direction and to break down. This breakdown period is marked by efforts to return to the original spirit, to the original charism. The institute's charism is studied, analyzed, described. Documents multiply. Organization is stressed, now not so much to facilitate normative behavior, as in the normative phase, as to promulgate a sense of purpose, a direction, the spirit of the community. Communications teams form, new constitutions are produced, meetings of formation personnel and of superiors are held. The aim is to recreate the original charism by teaching it, by indoctrination.

This is the "ideological phase," the phase of community meeting and study groups. The idea is this: What the charism did at the beginning, and what the normative structures did during the stable phase, ideology can do now. It does not work.

Most orders and congregations find themselves now in this ideological phase. We are learning that the charisms of our institutes cannot be renewed through norms and rules and guidelines. They will never be renewed through ideology either. Only the Holy Spirit can renew, in me and in my order or congregation, the charism of the institute.

Those cases where the Holy Spirit has begun to renew in power the charism of the institute have some common characteristics: spontaneity in sharing the things of the Spirit, power in apostolic activity, graces of prayer. In many ways, true renewal of the community's charism is a return to the first phase of the community's existence, the "spontaneous phase."

What can we do to help renew the charisms of our institutes, both in ourselves and in our orders and congregations as a whole? We can pray. And then, when the prayers begin to be answered by graces, we can cooperate with those graces.

Prayer for the Renewal of the Charism
of the Institute

Lord Jesus, renew me in the charism of my community. And renew my community in its particular charism.

Teach me to walk in your Spirit according to the particular vocation you have given me. I ask you now for the graces of prayer that are proper to the spirituality of my community. I do not know how to name those graces, what to call them; I am not sure even what I am asking you for. But you know, because you call me to these graces of prayer. Teach me to pray. And give me your gifts so that I can pray the way you want me to.

Help me in the work you give me to do, and let my poor and weak efforts be powerful in you for good. Let your power be made perfect in my weakness. Pour into my service the charismatic graces proper to my religious community. I do not ask to see the results, but I do ask that my labor be fruitful through the power of your Spirit.

Renew in me the gift of consecrated chastity and the gift of celibate community as you intend community to be lived in this institute. Renew in me the gift of poverty proper to the spirituality of my community. And renew me in my obedience to you through my institute; give me a greater share in the gift of obedience as we traditionally understand it in this community.

Lord Jesus, renew me. And renew my entire community in the graces of the life that you call us to. Amen.

Chapter Two

"BEHOLD,
I MAKE ALL THINGS NEW"

The three periods through which the charism of an institute passes—the "spontaneous phase" when the charism lives, the "normative phrase" when the charism's outlines are maintained by norms and structures, and the "ideological phase" in which attempts are made to revive the institute's charism through ideology, can be seen in broader perspective. These three phases of development correspond to the sociological stages of the normal evolution of any human community: an initial period of foundation and expansion, followed by a stable period in which the original spirit has been more or less institutionalized, followed in turn by a period of breakdown.

The Breakdown Period

When a religious community begins to break down, the institutional structures and belief systems that served it so well during its later expansion and during the stable period go through progressive dismantling, and the community's members face doubt, dissatisfaction, discouragement, anxiety, and stress. Unanswered questions about the institute's nature and purpose accumulate; tension increases; people leave; vocations drop. To confront the problems, standard remedies are applied, but the usual problem-solving methods prove ineffective. The community increasingly loses its sense of purpose and identity. Its members lack direction and lose hope in the community. The average age goes up almost a year every year. Some apostolic works are closed down, and people are overworked to support those works still going on. The decision-making and government process becomes more complex and often confused. Religious develop new interests, some compatible with the religious life, some not. Many no longer find sufficient meaning in traditional symbols, rules, and explanations. And many search for God in new ways, even turning to spiritual fads or political causes or pop psychology. It is not necessarily a time of moral decay in the religious life, although with the turmoil and confusion one might expect to find even serious moral lapses of various kinds.

As to the institute's charism, this is the ideological phase. Community leaders try to fill the void and to give direction by promulgating ideology based partly on the community's charism and partly on the need to respond to the signs of the times. But the efforts prove ineffective, and the community continues to break down.

Who is to blame for the breakdown? No one. It is a sociological phenomenon. This is just the way communities are founded, grow, stabilize, come apart. Theologically speaking, it seems simply to be the way the Holy Spirit acts, in concrete ways and in the midst of human sinfulness, with religious orders and congregations.

The Transition Period
Various authors—such as Raymond Fitz and Lawrence Cada, "The Recovery of the Religious Life," *Review for Religious* 34 (1975): 690-718; Bernard O'Connor, "The Future of Religious Life," *Supplement to Doctrine and Life* 18 (1978): 71-90—point out that historically, a community's breakdown period is followed by a period of transition. The transition stage has one of three possible outcomes: extinction, minimal survival, or revitalization. Extinction is the most common outcome, by far. Seventy-six percent of all men's religious orders founded before 1500 and sixty-four percent of those founded before 1800 have ceased to exist (Fitz and Cada, p. 705).

Most institutes that today find themselves in breakdown can reasonably expect to die. A few will go into a long period of low-level or minimal survival such as the Carthusians, the Camaldolese, and the Theatines, are in now. And a small percentage will become revitalized, will be made new, will be refounded and begin the cycle again: refoundation, expansion, stabilization, and so on.

In the past, several communities have finished one cycle,

ending in a breakdown period, and been refounded to begin a new three-phase cycle: for example, the Society of Jesus after its suppression, and the Franciscans and the Dominicans during the Counter-Reformation. Three characteristics mark all communities that in the past have survived the transition period through revitalization: (1) a strong response to the signs of the times; (2) a renewal of the charism of the institute; and (3) a profound renewal of prayer and of centeredness on Jesus Christ. Furthermore, in times in which the image of the religious life changes and in which new life-forms of consecration arise, the older communities undergoing revitalization take on some of the characteristics of the new communities (Fitz and Cada, p. 706).

If revitalization of the religious life interests us, then four questions arise immediately: (1) How can religious, singly and collectively, respond properly to the signs of today? (2) How can we renew the charisms of our institutes? (3) How can we bring about an increased spirit of prayer and of Christ-centeredness? (4) What new communities do we see forming today, and what can we learn from them for ourselves?

Signs of the times and the proper religious-life response to them differ, of course, according to time and place and according to the type of religious life in question. Maryknoll priests will not respond in the same way as cloistered Carmelite contemplative nuns. But where revitalization takes place, where real renewal happens, there will be some kind of positive response to changed conditions.

This means innovation in life-style and perhaps in apostolate. It calls for discernment in reading the signs of the times and in responding to them. This discernment will necessarily be according to the charism of the institute. Today's crises in the religious life demand graced discernment; human discernment alone will not work.

Graced discernment, charismatic discernment, depends on the inspiration of the Holy Spirit, and will take the form appropriate to the community's charism. So, in fact, the discernment required to respond to the signs of the times depends on the renewal of the institute's charism, of prayer, and of Christ-centeredness.

Renewal of the founding charism and renewal of the spirit of prayer go together. Right at the heart of every religious institute's charism are prayer and life centered on Jesus Christ. But this renewal cannot happen in a vacuum. Clearly it is not our work, but the Lord's. We cooperate with his work of renewing charisms, of bestowing the gift of prayer, and of centering us on himself. And he does these things by bringing about transforming changes—often by leading us through exterior changes of comportment that become the occasions of interior transformation through grace.

Today, when the image of the religious life has changed so much and continues to change, and when so many new communities are being founded, we can expect that what has happened before in similar periods of history will happen again: The religious communities that survive the breakdown and transition periods by entering a stage of revitalization will do so by assimilating appropriate elements and patterns from the new foundations.

Founding New Communities and Refounding Old Ones
The religious-life breakdown period began in the nineteen sixties. What new communities have been founded since then?

God's ways are surely not our ways. Nonetheless, we can look around and see what he is doing. We can search for and then observe the results of the Holy Spirit's action in founding new communities.

Some of the newly-founded communities that I know about are products of the Catholic Charismatic Renewal: for example, charismatic covenant communities such as the Hope community in New Jersey, the Come Follow Me religious community for men and women in the diocese of Trent, Italy, and the new charismatic monastic communities in France. Others, lay organizations such as the Focolarini, and some new diocesan congregations of women, are not directly connected with the Charismatic Renewal. But they all have in common certain qualities and characteristics that the religious life appears to need today for revitalization.

1. The new communities take seriously the power of the Spirit operating in their whole lives at both the individual and the group levels, especially in the areas of prayer and discernment. For example, their apostolic activities are determined not simply by the observed concrete needs, but by discerning—in the light of those needs—how the Holy Spirit is leading them.

2. They make explicit their brotherhood or sisterhood. Their members enter explicitly and responsibly into true covenantal relationship with one another. And they live out that covenant with the Lord and with one another in small-group face-to-face relationships.

3. In these small-group relationships, they freely share spiritual concerns, meeting regularly to pray together as the Spirit leads them and to share what the Lord is doing in their lives.

4. Their individual and corporate spiritual lives flow from an experience of new conversion of heart and of a new outpouring of the Holy Spirit's gifts proper to the vocation of each person.

Today, all over the world, the Holy Spirit is leading some religious men and women to do these same things. The future of the religious life depends on the Spirit working in those religious to refound what he began long ago.

Prayer for Guidance

Lord Jesus, send me your Holy Spirit. Renew me and kindle in me the new fire that you have to cast on the earth. Renew in me the charism of my institute. Give me a new outpouring of your Spirit, and renew in me your charismatic gifts of poverty, consecrated celibacy, and obedience.

Give me the gift of walking always in your Spirit of love and of light. Guide my steps. Show me what you call me to do.

Lead me to all with whom you call me to enter explicitly into covenant, to all with whom you call me to share spiritually.

Make me a part of the new temple you are building in the religious life. Amen.

Chapter Three

CHARISMS AND COMMUNITY

The letters of St. Paul contain a developed theology of Christian community, found especially in the first letter to the Corinthians and in the letters to the Romans and to the Ephesians. We can apply this theology to the religious life.

St. Paul's Theology of Christian Community
Paul understands the Church as the Body of Christ. The Church is not merely *like* the Body of Christ. In some mysterious way it *is* the Body of Christ. Paul speaks of the whole Church as Christ's Body, but also of the local church, of a single group, as the Body of Christ.

Why is this important for us? Because we can see each of our own groups as the Body of Christ. My order or congregation is the Body of Christ. My province, my monastery, is the Body of Christ. So I can look at what Paul says about Christian community as the Body of Christ and apply it to my own order, province, region, monastery.

Paul's theology of Christian community has four points developed in each of three key texts: Romans 12:1 to 13:7; Ephesians 4:4 to 6:9; and 1 Corinthians 12:12 to 14:40. We will work through these four points, taking one at a time.

1. Christian community is a unity. We are one thing, one because we form one Body of Christ. We have the same Spirit; we have received the same baptism; we share the same faith and the same hope (Rom. 12:4; Eph. 4:4-6; 1 Cor. 12:12-13).

2. But within this unity is a necessary diversity. The parts of the Body of Christ differ just as the parts of the human body differ; and the parts of the Body of Christ are interdependent, need one another, just as the parts of the human body need one another. The hand is not the foot; the eye is not the ear. A human body that was just a big foot, or only a monstrous eye, would be horrible. And the hands and the feet need each

other; the eyes and the ears depend on each other. The body's organs are differentiated according to their various functions, and each complements the others, because together they make up the one body.

So too in the Christian community. Each member has different gifts and so a different role; yet all the members are important, and the body needs them all.

However, St. Paul does not mean to refer here to natural gifts, nor even to gifts of grace in a general way. Although most translations have the words *gift* and *gifts,* Paul in the original Greek writes "*charisma*" and "*charismata*"— "charism" and "charisms." And even though Paul does not mean what we mean today by charism every time he uses the word, he does in these texts. He means a special gift, given to some but not to all, for some useful service. It is evident from the examples he gives that Paul means what we mean by "charisms."

Each of the three texts we are studying lists various charisms. The lists differ because the situations and the immediate needs of the three communities—at Rome, at Ephesus, at Corinth—differed. In the letter to the group at Rome, Paul lists examples of different charisms: prophecy, ministering to others, teaching, exhorting, almsgiving, presiding at an assembly or over the community, performing works of mercy. Prosaic though most of these gifts may be, they are, for Paul and for the early Church, quite clearly special *gifts* from the Lord, and gifts *before* they are roles to be filled.

The letter to the Ephesians has a somewhat different list of charisms, naming categories of people who do special things rather than naming the gifts themselves: apostles, prophets, evangelists, shepherds, and teachers. On the other hand, the first letter to the church at Corinth contains several lists of charisms, and all of them, by comparison with the lists of the other two letters, would seem a little exotic to most people today, at least to those outside some form of charismatic renewal. This is because, as becomes evident in the letter, Paul addresses himself to the specific Corinthian problem of order in the prayer assembly. Therefore he mentions for the most part the gifts used in the prayer assembly; they are, of course, the same gifts used in charismatic prayer meetings: speaking words of wisdom, "word of knowledge," a faith that "moves mountains," healings, miracles, prophecy, the discernment of good and evil spirits, prophecy in tongues and interpreting such prophetic utterances (1 Cor. 12:8-10; see the lists in 12:28, 12:29-30, and 13:6). The Corinthians, apparently, tended to overdo prophesying in tongues and not to wait for inspired interpretations of what was said in tongues, with the chaotic results that Paul describes in chapter fourteen.

A great diversity of charisms, then, exists within the unity of the one Body of Christ. And now Paul returns to talk about what animates, gives life to, each of the charisms and the Body as a whole.

3. Without love, the user of even the most spectacular gifts is nothing, and the best speaking in tongues is just noise (1 Cor. 13:1-3). Love is long-suffering, kind, not jealous or boastful or proud, is respectful, unselfish, not irritable, does not hold a grudge (1 Cor. 13:4-6). Paul counsels the Ephesians to "be kind and compassionate to one another, pardoning one another as God in Christ has pardoned you" (Eph. 4:32 RF), and to "live in love" (Eph. 5:2 RF). He advises the Romans to love one another without pretense, warmly; to honor and defer to one another, to show zeal, fervor, and hospitality; to bless even people who curse them and persecute them; to live in humility; and as far as possible to live in peace with everyone (Rom. 12:9-18).

Beginning with the idea of unity in the Body of Christ, Paul has moved to the theme of diversity of charisms and then goes on to exhort the three communities to "live in love."

4. Finally, Paul comes to the topic of order and harmony. To the Corinthians, he preaches order in the assembly of prayer, giving particular ground rules and procedures regarding the use of the charisms of prophecy and tongues and of interpretation (1 Cor. 14). To the Romans, he talks about civil order and good relations between the Church and the state (Rom. 13:1-7). And to the Ephesians, Paul speaks about domestic order: between husband and wife, children and parents, servants and masters (Eph. 5:22 to 6:9).

It is important to note that order is the last point, and that it follows from unity, diversity of charisms, and love. If Christians remain united in Christ, respecting and using the charisms he gives through his Spirit, loving one another in service, then order and harmony will flow from that love within the Body of Christ simply as an expression of that love in the various concrete circumstances of life.

The Ideal for the Religious Life

Let us apply Paul's theology to our own orders, congregations, provinces, monasteries, and larger (e.g., university) communities. Then we will be able to see how we do or do not measure up to the ideal and what we might do about it. But first, the ideal:

Each order, congregation, province, monastery, large local community, is Christ's Body. As such, it is a unit, has a substance and consistency, an identity.

Each of these units contains a diversity of charisms. The Holy Spirit becomes manifest, as the power of the Lord's love, through the charisms; the power of God becomes, so to speak, visible and tangible in the gifts of the Spirit. The particular cluster of charisms that makes up the "charism" of a particular congregation is in evidence in every member. And beyond that, each formed member has his or her own charism or charisms, and is to use them in his or her particular apostolate.

Love informs this unity-in-diversity. Love makes the religious group go, gives it life.

And love making itself concrete in everyday life creates order and harmony at every level.

Evaluation of the Religious Life Today in the Light of the Ideal

Starting from the last point and working backward, I think many of us, perhaps most or even all of us, can say that yes, there is a certain harmony in our community lives. And yes, there is love in our communities—not perfect, and not perfectly expressed, lived with faults and failures. But we *have* experienced love in our communities. So much for the fourth and the third points.

The trouble starts with the second point: the charisms.

Charisms can certainly be found in our communities. But do we find the full spectrum of charisms or the power we might expect? In many cases, most perhaps, the answer is no.

But what is the real question? Is it a question of reforming the whole of religious life for men and women, of somehow converting and "charismaticizing" every religious sister, brother, and priest? If that is the question, then we have a right to be discouraged, because things look hopeless: We will all be dead before that happens.

I suggest that it is not a question of reforming the whole religious life, of reforming every man and woman religious, of forming some kind of "charismatic community" with every person in my province or house or monastery.

I propose that it is not a question of somehow "reforming everyone," but of *some religious living the religious life, somehow together, in an increasingly charismatic way.* And we can do this now.

Prayer for the Grace to Live Community
in the Spirit of Jesus

Teach me, Lord, to live in community according to your plan for me, to live in your Holy Spirit in a more charismatic way. Increase in me all the charisms of my apostolate, of my personal prayer, and of my life in community.

Teach me to live in love, by the power of your Holy Spirit who is Love. Lead me, Lord, along your path of loving and humble service—not only service of those outside the community but also of those with whom I live.

And teach me, Lord, to live in the power of the love you pour into my heart through your Holy Spirit. Empower me, Lord, to live community. Amen.

Chapter Four

THE CROSS AND THE CHARISM OF POVERTY

Poverty can be considered as a vow, as an interior psychological state, or as a gift. Religious poverty at the most profound level is a special gift from the Lord *before* it can be a response to the Lord's love. It is precisely this gift, this charism, that empowers me to respond to the Lord's love by living my commitment in poverty.

Poor with Jesus Poor

The gospel text about the rich young man refers to the counsel of poverty and stands as the classically cited passage concerning the vow of poverty. "Jesus said to him: 'If you would be perfect, go, sell what you possess and give to the poor, and you will have treasure in heaven; and come, follow me'" (Mt. 19:21 RSV).

This fits with Jesus' general teaching on poverty as a Christian value: "Do not lay up for yourselves treasures on earth, where moth and rust consume and where thieves break in and steal, but lay up for yourselves treasures in heaven. . . . For where your treasure is, there will your heart be also" (Mt. 6:19-20 RSV); "It is easier for a camel to pass through the eye of a needle than for a rich man to enter the kingdom of heaven" (Mt. 19:24 RSV); "The kingdom of heaven is like a treasure hidden in a field which someone has found; he hides it, and goes off happy, and sells everything he owns and buys that field" (Mt. 13:44 JB).

The most important words in Jesus' invitation to the rich young man are "Come, follow me," and they should be understood in the context of Jesus' teaching on discipleship. "If anyone wants to be a follower of mine, let him renounce himself and take up his cross and follow me. For anyone who wants to save his life will lose it, but anyone who loses his life for my sake will find it" (Mt. 16:24-25 JB).

The Christian virtue of poverty, then, consists of renouncing self, taking up the cross, and following Jesus. But beyond this general call is another call, a call to go further and to give more. This call Jesus addressed to the rich young man. Like all Jesus' invitations, it both calls and empowers one to respond. The power to answer the call to a radical poverty, to a special following of Jesus on the way of the cross, is the charism of poverty. Not all Christians are called to this kind of poverty, to this radical way of being poor with Jesus poor. But some are. And the power to live out the answer to that call is the charism of poverty.

As a charism, poverty enables me to serve the Lord with a special freedom. I am free to serve him in an apostolate that earns a good salary, or a small one, or that earns nothing at all. Money and material advantages do not determine my choices in serving the Lord. And so the charism of poverty "builds up the body of Christ" in that it frees me more for service. And further, it relates me in a particular way to Jesus, making me his disciple in chosen radical poverty, in the poverty of the cross.

When Jesus dies on Calvary he has nothing. Not only does he die without any material possessions at all, but he dies stripped of all honor, of all dignity, of all respect. He dies not like a common criminal but more shamefully, like an uncommon criminal; not only rejected by his own people, but hanging on a hill outside the city gate, cut off from human society.

Subjected to extensive and horribly severe torture, both physical and psychological, he finally dies without composure, without a vestige of human dignity, feeling utterly abandoned even by God and crying out to God, "Why have you abandoned me?" The gospel accounts of Jesus' death are strikingly laconic. The Church had no crucifixes for hundreds of years, until the shock could be assimilated, the shock of the terribleness of Jesus' death.

So too, the charism of poverty takes me beyond just material poverty freely chosen, lived out voluntarily. The charism of poverty associates me intimately with Jesus in his passion and death, crucifying me to the world and the world to me (see Gal. 6:14). "I have been crucified with Christ" (Gal. 2:19). It frees me from ambition for honors, for applause, for attention from others. The charism of poverty acts as an antidote for that malady that has beset professionally religious people since the scribes and the Pharisees and before: the need for narcissistic feedback.

The charism of poverty empowers me to be poor with Jesus poor, poor materially and poor interiorly, stripped of everything, for love of Jesus who calls me. Religious poverty is not, then, some kind of stoical pragmatism, a streamlining for service. It does free me for service, but beyond that and more importantly, it relates me in love to Jesus who laid down his life for me.

Poverty and Liberation

One of the fruitful insights of Latin American theology of liberation is that religious poverty frees me to become one with those who live in oppressive poverty; it enables me to enter into solidarity with the downtrodden, the suffering, the poor, the marginal people who, with Jesus, are "outside the city," outside respectable human society. I can see Jesus in them, the least of his brothers and sisters. And, united intimately in love with Jesus, I enter into solidarity with the most oppressed, the poorest, the most marginal of his brothers and sisters. I find Jesus most clearly and distinctly in the most needy—in the retarded, in prisoners, in the very ill whether physically or mentally or both, in the outcasts and the severely troubled and poorest of the poor. Not that entering into solidarity with those who have nothing is my *motive* for living poverty. The motive is love. The motive is Jesus, who calls me in love to respond to his love for me. This loving response, made in the power of his Spirit, leads me to live out religious poverty, and it leads me to a preference for the poor.

The gospel preference for the poor stands at the heart of Jesus' teaching; it runs through the Acts of the Apostles and Paul's letters; and it holds the thematic center of the letter of James. In his public life Jesus goes to the oppressed, eats with whores and publicans, heals the sick, raises up those who are brought low. This gospel preference for the poor is, always, an apostolic priority. To be poor with Jesus means to be poor with the least of his brothers and sisters so as to participate in Jesus' mission of redemption, a mission he always understood as applying to this life as well as to the next. "He has sent me to bring the good news to the poor, to proclaim freedom to captives and recovering of sight to the blind, to set free the downtrodden..." (Lk. 4:18 RF). I go to Jesus in the poor and the needy and the oppressed because the charism of poverty empowers me to give up everything for him, because I am free to love him and to serve him in the downtrodden, the outcasts, the marginal people.

This freedom that the charism of poverty gives me is above all an *interior* freedom. It takes the form of a radical, thoroughgoing dependence on God, a dependence that looks to the Lord for salvation, for liberation from present difficulties both for myself and for those whom the Lord has called me to serve.

The theology of liberation has not always in the past recognized the primacy of poverty of spirit, of that interior freedom that has the shape of a total dependence on the Lord. God does save his people, bring them out of bondage, redeem them. But this deliverance and this redemption begin, on the part of the people, with crying out to the Lord, with a desperate recourse to the only one who can truly save.

The Old Testament event of the Exodus dominates Israel's theology of salvation. God frees his people, now and always, just as he did then. And the deliverance from the Egyptian bondage begins not with political commitment, nor with education, nor with the solidarity of the oppressed, but with the interior poverty that cries out to the Lord. One of the Bible's oldest passages, directions and a prayer for the temple offering of the first fruits of the harvest, goes like this:

> The priest shall take the basket from your hand, and set it down before the altar of the Lord your God.
>
> And you shall make response before the Lord your God, saying, "A wandering Aramean was my father; and he went down into Egypt and sojourned there, few in number; and there he became a nation, great, mighty, and populous. And the Egyptians treated us harshly and afflicted us, and laid upon us harsh bondage. Then we cried out to the Lord the God of our fathers, and the Lord heard our voice, and saw our affliction, our toil, and our oppression; and the

Lord brought us out of Egypt with a mighty hand and an outstretched arm, with great terror, with signs and wonders; and he brought us into this place and gave us this land, a land flowing with milk and honey. And behold, now I bring the first of the fruit of the ground, which you, O Lord, have given me." (Deut. 26:4-11 RF)

The New Testament event analogous to the Exodus and its fulfillment is the death and resurrection of Jesus. Jesus' deliverance from the powers of darkness is his passage from death to risen life. This passage has its beginning in his crying out to the Father, "My God, my God, why have you abandoned me?" (Mt. 27:46). Jesus uses the opening line of Psalm 22 as a prayer to express his feeling of being abandoned by the Father, as a prayer of lamentation, an expression of profound poverty, of radical dependence on the Father. As a lament, Jesus' prayer expresses not only his own feeling of being abandoned, but also—implicitly—his abandonment into the hands of the Father. Jesus' prayer of crying out to the Lord comes just before his death; in Matthew's carefully chosen words Jesus "yielded up his spirit" to the Father, and in Luke's account Jesus cries in a loud voice, "Father, into your hands I commend my spirit."

This abandonment into the Father's hands is the essence of interior poverty. The charism of religious poverty gives me the power to surrender to God, to say yes to the Father with Jesus, and in and through him.

Jesus' whole life finds its summation and meaning in his death on the cross, because his death, like his life, was a surrender, a yes to the Father. "Jesus Christ . . . was not Yes and No; but in him it is always Yes. For all the promises of God find their Yes in him. That is why we say the Amen through him, to the glory of God" (2 Cor. 1:19-20 RSV).

Prayer for the Gift of Poverty

Lord Jesus, I ask you for a new fullness of the charism of poverty. I ask you to reveal to me my inordinate attachments, my holding on to things or to persons, my "richness" that keeps me from saying a more complete yes to you.

I surrender to you my excessive search for material comforts, and whatever material goods I have that I do not really need to serve you.

I surrender to you my excessive need for attention, for acclaim and applause, for narcissistic feedback from others. I surrender all my selfish ambitions, my search for honors, my vainglory and my pride.

I surrender to you my possessiveness of those whom I love; teach me to love (mention the names of any person or persons that you tend to be attached to in a selfish or possessive way) freely, leaving others free; teach me to love with an open hand. I renounce the possessiveness in my love for others; teach me to love more and better.

And I ask you now for new graces, for new power to live for you, for a new outpouring of the charism of religious poverty.

Give me the interior poverty that depends on you and not on the world's acceptance. You say to me now, "If the world hates you, know that it has hated me before it hated you. If you were of the world, the world would love its own; but because you are not of the world, but I chose you out of the world, therefore the world hates you. Remember the word that I spoke to you, A servant is not greater than his master" (Jn. 15:18-20 RSV).

Teach me, Lord, to enter by the narrow gate that leads to life (Mt. 7:13-14). You are that gate, Lord; let me follow you, taking up my cross.

For you alone, Lord, are my portion. I have no inheritance, for you are my inheritance; I want no possessions, for you are my possession (Ezek. 44:28). Amen.

Obedience is an aspect of teachability.

Chapter Five

MARTYRDOM AND THE CHARISM OF OBEDIENCE

"He goes before them, and the sheep follow him, for they know his voice" (Jn. 10:4 RSV). The charism of religious obedience empowers me to hear Jesus' voice and to follow him. In more juridical words, the gift of obedience gives me the power to fulfill the obligation of my vow of obedience; that obligation is to hear Jesus' voice and to follow him. My obedience to Jesus shares in Jesus' obedience to the Father. Just as Jesus looks to the Father ("I know the Father"—Jn. 10:15 RSV), I look to Jesus ("My own know me"—Jn. 10:14 RSV). In following Jesus, I obey the Father, and my obedience is a share in Jesus' obedience. This, then, is the gift he gives me in the charism of obedience: to follow him, sharing in his obedience to the Father.

Jesus' Obedience and Our Obedience
Conceived by the power of the Holy Spirit (Lk. 1:35), anointed by the Spirit for mission at his baptism, Jesus lives out that mission "led by the Spirit" (Lk 4:1 RSV) and "in the power of the Spirit" (Lk. 4:14 RSV). "The Spirit of the Lord is upon me, because he has anointed me" (Lk. 4:18 RSV). Jesus' ministry manifests the power of his Spirit and shows that the kingdom of God has come (Lk. 11:20). Jesus' obedience to his Father, lived out in Jesus' mission, is inspired, guided, and vitalized by the Holy Spirit.

Jesus' mission, which he undertook in obedience to the Father, culminates in his passion and death. This is clear even at the beginning of Jesus' ministry, when he is baptized and anointed for mission. "When Jesus had been baptized and was praying, the heaven was opened, and the Holy Spirit descended upon him in bodily form as a dove, and a voice came from heaven, 'You are my beloved son; in you I am well pleased'" (Lk. 3:22 RSV, adapted).

"You are my beloved son" refers to Abraham's willingness to sacrifice his beloved son Isaac on the mountain (Gen. 22:2). And the rest of the Father's words to Jesus, "in you I am well pleased," refer to the Suffering Servant of the book of Isaiah—"in whom I am well pleased; I have endowed him with my spirit" (Is. 42:1 RF). Jesus' own baptism-for-mission looks forward to that other "baptism with which I must be baptized" (Lk. 12:50 RF), his passion and death.

Jesus' obedience to the Father consists in this: He *hears* the Father and *does his will*. "I can do nothing on my own authority; as I hear, I judge; and my judgment is just because I seek not my own will but the will of him who has sent me" (Jn. 5:30 RSV).

Jesus was obedient to the Father "even unto death." This obedience of Jesus to the Father takes the form of an "emptying out" of self, of a *kenosis*. It begins with the Incarnation, "taking the form of a servant," and Nativity, "being born in human likeness" and living "in human form." Jesus "became obedient unto death, even death on a cross" (Phil. 2:7-8 RF).

In other words, at his Incarnation Jesus entered into the world completely, by being born into it, being "made like his brothers and sisters in every respect," "partaking of the same nature," so that he might be "made perfect through suffering," and through his death save and free us (Heb. 2:14-17). Having entered into the world by his Incarnation, Jesus went even further into the world by his death on the cross. By his obedience, he descended into the heart of the world so that, risen, he could be the Heart of the world.

The obedience of the religious to Jesus participates in Jesus' obedience to the Father. Religious obedience is a special way of following Jesus by taking up the cross and entering into the world. It is not a flight from the world and from the world's responsibilities; it is an entering more deeply into the world by going in a total and direct way to Jesus who has become the Heart of the world. Religious obedience calls for a radical self-emptying in imitation of Jesus, for a radical renunciation—not a renunciation so as to leave the world, but a renunciation that is a freeing and a streamlining so as to go further into the world by going to the world's Heart who is Jesus. Seen in this perspective, even the most secluded contemplative life is not a fleeing from the world; on the contrary, it marks the most complete and radical entry into the Heart of the world.

Obedience and Martyrdom

In the early Church, popular belief held that Jesus was the first martyr. The Christian martyr shares in the martyrdom of Jesus and lives even to death, as Jesus did, the meaning and the values of the cross. In an age of religious anomie, the Christian martyr dies not so much in defense of the faith as in witness to Christian values. Christianity itself, judged irrelevant, seems not worth persecuting. But its values often menace the ethical systems of modern groups and societies. Martyrdom gives Christianity's values credibility.

The Church has always witnessed through its martyrs, from the apostles down through Ignatius of Antioch, Joan of Arc, Thomas More, Oliver Plunkett, Charles Luanga, and Maximilian Kolbe. But never, not even in the early Church, has this witness been so universal. Christians are being killed for their Christian faith even as I write this and even as you read it, in many countries in Latin America, in several countries in black Africa, and in many other places on this globe. And for every well-known martyr like Archbishop Romero and the three American religious women with the lay missionary in El Salvador, there are hundreds and even thousands of martyrs whose witness is less widely known but just as real.

What about the political factor? Are those who die today, even though they die for Christian values and because they live their faith, really martyrs? Do they not die, always or nearly always, in some political context, whether that of Communist totalitarianism or of some other type of political oppression or violent confrontation? Does not the political dimension of their deaths invalidate those deaths as true martyrdoms?

No. From the beginning, starting with the crucifixion of Jesus, martyrdom has often had a strong political dimension. In Roman theocracy, Christians died for not offering incense to the emperor. Joan of Arc burned to death in an awful mixture of ecclesiastical and national politics. Thomas More was beheaded for opposing the King of England. And Jesus himself, crucified under Pontius Pilate and by Roman soldiers, suffered and died in an occupied country in which the local religious leaders and the occupation government each strove to serve their own interests while accommodating the interests of the others, no matter what moral compromise might be involved.

> Every believer who deliberately accepts the extreme consequences of his baptismal promises and who, following Christ's example, is ready to give witness of his love for God and for mankind even to death, depending not on his own strength but on the Holy Spirit who makes his witness authentic, is *disposed to martyrdom*. And whoever meets a violent death in living out his baptismal promises and gives, as Christ gave, proof of great love by dying for those whom he loves (Jn. 15:13) is truly a *martyr* (André Rayez et al., eds., *Dictionnaire de Spiritualité* [Paris: Beauchesne, 1980] 10:733; cf. St. Thomas Aquinas, *Summa Theologica*, II-II, q. 1, a. 5).

Martyrdom is a charism, a special gift given to some, but not to all, for the building up of Christ's body the Church. And it shares in Jesus' own martyrdom, participates in Jesus' obedience to the Father "even unto death." Martyrdom is the ultimate form and the great symbol of the obedience to God to which we are all called. And the martyrdom of a religious is not only a new gift from the Lord to both the religious and the Church, but the outcome and direct extension of the religious martyr's vow and charism of obedience.

Just as martyrdom is a form of obedience, so too religious obedience is analogous to martyrdom. Both the religious and the martyr, sharing in Jesus' total self-emptying and self-giving in love, enter with Jesus into the heart of the world to become with him the Heart of the world. Both the charism of religious obedience and the charism of martyrdom stand for the total dependence of all persons on God and for the obedience to

God to which each person is called. They represent the funda- ✓
mental relation of every person to God.

Both martyrdom and religious obedience give basically the ✓
same kind of witness: to the values represented by the cross of
Jesus. Most contemporary cultures regard religious values
with indifference, partly because those values are not clearly
represented and not adequately witnessed to. Both martyrdom and religious obedience define and proclaim the values
that Jesus' crucifixion stands for: primarily, *freedom*. ✓

In particular, religious obedience frees me from the Law.
The charism of religious obedience frees me from slavery to the
Law by empowering me to fulfill the Law and to go beyond it.
St. Paul, in chapter 7 of his letter to the Romans, explains this
freedom in terms of the Jewish Law. Without Christ, we have
the Law but not the capacity to live up to its demands. I know I
should live the Law but find that I cannot, and so the knowledge of the Law only increases my responsibility and therefore
my guilt. That is, the Law multiplies sin. I live in interior
conflict between what I am (a sinner) and what I ought to be
(faithful to the Law). I tend, therefore, to reject what I am and
deny I am a sinner; this proves ineffective and solves nothing.
So, to escape the conflict, I reject what I ought to be; I reject
the Law; I sin even more, and again sin is multiplied through
the Law. I am alienated now not only from myself through sin,
but also from the Law through disobedience.

We can enlarge Paul's teaching on the Jewish Law to include
all ethical norms and systems. Any ethical system that contains
only human values is in the end insufficient. Without the Spirit
of Jesus, I lack the capacity not only to live according to
Christian precepts but even to follow valid ethical systems or
laws. All law, without the capacity to follow it, without a power
that comes from the Spirit of Christ, tends to lead to disobedience and to the rejection of law. This is the human condition,
the human dilemma, and the reason I need Christ not only for
salvation but even to be truly human.

The resolution of the conflict between knowing the law and
being incapable of living according to the law comes about
through living in union with Jesus Christ according to the

Spirit. What law cannot do because human nature is weak, God does in and for me. By Jesus' death on the cross, my slavery to sin, to breaking the law, comes to an end; a new order is created, the order of God's grace and of life in the Spirit. By his death on the cross, Jesus has created a new situation in which I need no longer be alienated from myself by sinning, need no longer be disobedient, alienated from the law, because now I can live in Christ, free from the law.

This freedom does not mean that I can break the law, that I am permitted to sin. It means that my new life in the Spirit of Jesus transcends the law, goes beyond it. I am free from law so that now I can obey God's law which is more, not less, than human law. I now can have the freedom of the children of God. And I am freed from general disobedience, not by simply accepting the ethical values of human society but by going beyond them to obey the law of the Spirit.

Obedience as Hearing and Doing
What specifically does the grace, the charism, of religious obedience enable me to do? It gives me the power to listen lovingly to what the Lord is saying to me. It gives me the power to lay down my life daily for the Lord, by trying in love to do and to live what I hear him say to me.

How does the Lord speak to me? Through my prayer; through Scripture; through all the events of my life; through other people; through my apostolate; through my problems, trials, difficulties, successes; and in a special way through the Church, particularly through my congregation and my superiors.

Prayer for the Gift of Obedience

Lord Jesus, help me to hear you better and to live in obedience to your loving will for me.

Give me a great increase in the charism of obedience according to the spirit of my institute so that I may follow you in the way for which you have chosen me, so that I may not shrink from the cross but carry it in union with you.

Help me, through a new outpouring of the charism of obedience into my heart and my will, to obey your loving will always and to live in a spirit of listening and of readiness to hear your word and do it.

Give me a greater spirit of surrender, that I may say yes to you in all things, laying down my life daily for love of you.

Give me your grace of being obedient even unto death, and to live that same kenosis, that same emptying out, that you lived so that I may be filled with your light and your Spirit.

Let me live your "emptying out," Lord, in my daily contemplation in humble and loving reverence. Let me live it in my community and in my apostolate in reverent service and in obedience to you in all the ways you speak to me. Let me live it in my death, however you call me to come to you finally. Amen.

Chapter Six

THE EUCHARIST
AND THE CHARISM OF CHASTITY

All Christians are called to practice the Christian virtue of chastity according to their state of life. The chastity that religious men and women formally profess is traditionally called "consecrated chastity."

Consecrated chastity, like poverty and obedience, is above all, before it is a vow or an obligation, a charism. Like any other charism, consecrated chastity is both a call from God and the means to respond to that call. Like other charisms, it frees me for serving, for building up the Body of Christ. And because a charism is a gift from God—given to some who are chosen for it, not given to all—consecrated chastity is primarily a special way of relating to the Giver, a new way of being in Jesus.

As a charism, consecrated chastity is a gift given only to those who are chosen for it ("He who is able to receive this, let him receive it"), a gift for service ("for the Kingdom"—Mt. 19:12 RSV), and a special way of being united to the Lord ("each has his own charism"—1 Cor. 7:7 RF).

This is not a new idea, but it has been neglected by theologians. The recent vast theological literature on celibacy has been often polemic, arguing for or against a necessarily celibate priesthood. This juridical approach to the subject stands in the same line as the canonical approaches to the vow of chastity that were prevalent in the religious life before the Second Vatican Council. Since the Council, much attention has focused on the psychological aspects of consecrated chastity. This recent overemphasis on the psychological has had, as one might have expected, deplorable results. Consecrated celibacy is primarily a phenomenon of faith; approaches to it that try to reflect on the total phenomenon while neglecting that truth are at best unfortunate, whether those approaches are juridical or psychological. Without the faith dimension which properly belongs to theology, juridical reflection on celibacy becomes legalism, and psychological reflection becomes simultaneously Pelagian and pessimistic about the possibility of perfect chastity. For consecrated celibacy is a special grace, a gift from God; it calls for dependence on the power of the Holy Spirit because it is a charism.

The Consecrated Person as Sacred

What does the charism of consecrated chastity mean? What is consecrated chastity? What does it mean to be celibate for Jesus and for the kingdom? To begin with, what does it mean to be consecrated?

We call a person consecrated, or somehow sacred, when that person has a sacred mission or function or vocation—a mission, function, or vocation that in some way refers directly to God. The word *consecrated* means set apart as *sacred.* The words *sacred* and *consecrated* refer not to quality of being—such as the word *holiness* for example—but to *role in life,* to vocation, to mission. The Church is sacred because of its divine mission: to be the vehicle of salvation for humanity through its ministry of word and sacrament. The holiness of the Church in a particular place and at a given moment in history is one thing; the Church's sacred mission, and so its sacredness, is another. Again, a chalice used in the Mass is sacred because of its function. It is used in an activity that refers directly to God. A church building is sacred because of its function, use, or role. A priest is a consecrated or sacred person not because of some personal quality, such as holiness, but because his priestly calling—to preach the word and to give the sacraments—has direct reference to God, is sacred. A religious is sacred, a consecrated person, because his or her mission is one of direct, active witness to the kingdom of God. The mission, function, role of a religious to witness to the presence and to the coming of the kingdom consecrates the religious because it is sacred, refers directly to God. In short, the priest and the religious are "set aside" for God; they belong to God by reason of their vocation.

The word *secular* also refers to role or vocation or function. Civil government has a properly secular mission and secular

- 40 -

function. A coffee cup is secular because it is used for a secular (non-sacred) purpose. A public library, by reason of its function, is a secular institution. Whatever does not refer directly to God in vocation or role or use is secular. In this way, a human being, precisely as a human being, is sacred because he or she has been created for God. By his or her very vocation as human, a person is structured to know and love God directly, pointed to a supernatural destiny as the purpose and fulfillment of his or her human nature. But in his or her mission in this world a Christian may well be a layperson, secular.

Consecrated chastity, then, is chastity that refers directly to God. The purpose of consecrated chastity is to give oneself in a special way to God; furthermore, the witness value of that chastity refers directly to God and to the kingdom of God.

Consecration and Love
Taken simply in itself, apart from the idea of consecration, chastity is a loss. It means giving up some of the possibilities of the fulfillment of what it means to be a man or a woman. The consecrated celibate gives up those possibilities of the fulfillment of his manhood or her womanhood that consist in being a husband or wife and a father or mother, for example. Consecrated chastity, of course, does not mean giving up one's sexual instinct. But it does mean giving up all voluntary use of that instinct. Consecrated chastity, then, means non-fulfillment of the sexual side of one's nature. It is true that a celibate can find progressive fulfillment as a person in other ways—especially through growing intimacy with God, and through friendship and union in some kind of community. But this does not suppress the loss of fulfillment in the sexual sphere.

A person who is celibate for God and for the sake of the kingdom, a consecrated celibate, accepts this loss. He or she is aware of personal feelings and motives for action; when these come from sexual instinct, they are irrelevant to his or her life. He or she may hear the voice of sexual instinct but does not listen to it. He or she accepts the loss of sexual fulfillment and the aloneness that goes with that loss.

What justifies the celibacy of a consecrated person? The

justification is this: Celibacy is chosen precisely as a means of consecration. It becomes a way of giving oneself to the Lord and, in the Lord, to others. Consecrated celibacy, in other words, is a charism. It involves a loss that is not suppressed or made up for or in some way fulfilled at a spiritual level; but it is a loss that is more than justified for those whom the Lord calls. It is a way of greater self-giving, and so a way to love more.

Consecration through celibacy, then, is much more than simply abstention from sexual activity. It is a self-giving to God. The problem with even talking about consecrated celibacy is that we can tend to discuss it as if it were some kind of commodity, a thing. In reality, it is not celibacy that is consecrated, but the person—and celibacy is a means to an end. The Lord calls a person not so much to celibacy as to himself. It is not celibacy that is the center of a consecrated life, nor consecration; it is Jesus.

The celibate life is a life primarily of love. Consecrated chastity is a means to free the consecrated person for greater love of God and of everyone. How can this life of love be sustained? Like any life of love, it needs a central relationship of intimate love, a relationship that sustains and organizes and gives life to all the other relationships in one's life. This central relationship of intimate love is with the Lord.

For this reason, the consecrated life does not stop short of the fulfillment that can be found in marriage. It gives up the fulfillment found in marriage in order to go further. Certainly married persons singly and together can experience union with Jesus. But the charism of consecrated chastity, like the charisms of poverty and obedience, enables a more single-minded devotion to the Lord.

Christian marriage is a sacrament, a mystery, and a symbol of a higher reality. The mystery of marriage lies in this: Marriage symbolizes the union between Jesus Christ and his Church (Eph. 5:32). This union between Jesus and his Church will be consummated, completed, at the end of time, in the fulfillment of the world to come. Therefore there will be no "giving and taking in marriage" in the next world, because the symbol—marriage—will have passed into the reality, the complete union of the Church with Jesus.

Consecration through celibate chastity short-circuits the symbol of Jesus' union with his Church to go around and beyond the symbol straight to the reality: direct union with Jesus through a total giving of self to God in this life. Consecrated celibacy goes beyond sacramental symbolism to the reality. The reason why it is not a sacrament is that it is more—not less—than sacramental. It is a kind of "supersacrament."

Going beyond the sacramental symbolism of the marriage state, celibate consecration anticipates the end of history and the beginning of the New Jerusalem. And so the consecrated person stands as an eschatological sign. Christian marriage symbolizes sacramentally the union between Jesus and the Church, not only as that union exists now but also as it will be at the end of time, at the eschatological wedding feast of the Lord and his Church when he comes a second time to signal this world's end and the beginning of the world he has inaugurated by his resurrection. But celibate consecration to the Lord brings that eschatological wedding feast into the present on an individual scale—not symbolically but in a way that is real even if mysterious; celibate consecration means a union that exists not in symbol but in fact, even though in faith.

Consecrated Chastity and the Lordship of Jesus
Consecration through religious chastity professes and proclaims the lordship of Jesus. This profession and proclamation of Jesus' lordship takes place through the living out of celibate consecration as a total bringing of oneself under the lordship of Jesus.

What is the meaning of the lordship of Jesus for me? Besides recognizing Jesus' lordship over everything, I am called to recognize Jesus as my own personal Lord. Just as the Lord Jesus gives meaning and existence to the whole world, so he gives me my personal meaning and existence. Just as all history finds its true meaning and its fulfillment in Jesus, so I find my own true meaning and fulfillment in him. Jesus risen is actually present in all of history and in the whole universe, and he is actively present in my whole personal history and in every part of my life. I find my personal value, meaning, existence, and fulfillment in the risen Jesus. And just as the Father's plan from the beginning of time has been to recapitulate all things in Christ, to unify and reconcile everything in Jesus, so too the Father's plan is and has always been to unify and reconcile everything in my being and in my life in Jesus, to integrate me, to give me personal unity, to knit up the frazzled parts of myself, in and through and under the lordship of Jesus.

Jesus calls me not only to accept his love and lordship but to participate actively in the Father's plan to recapitulate all things in himself. Jesus invites me to bring everything in my life to him, to put everything in my life under his lordship: my worries, my problems, my anxieties and fears, my failures, my successes, my hopes for myself and for others—everything. I can take each preoccupation, every burden, all difficulties and joys and sorrows to Jesus, placing them under his loving lordship.

We can look at the lordship of Jesus from a slightly different point of view, in terms of the orientation of all things to the risen Jesus. The essence of something can be defined only by what that thing finally becomes. The essential identity of a person can be determined only by what that person is destined to become. Now, everything and every person is oriented toward its final consummation and fulfillment in the risen Jesus. Every creature finds its true meaning and direction in Jesus. This orientation of all things to Jesus is what we mean when we say Jesus is Lord.

The essence of anything, and the identity of any person, is determined by that thing's or that person's relation to Jesus— because he is the final judge who assigns to each its final post, its ultimate meaning, and who will in the end illuminate its existence utterly. So we are not yet what God has destined us to be from the beginning; we do not yet possess our true identities. Each of us is becoming, is in the process toward becoming our true self. This becoming is a relationship with Jesus. In the Book of Revelation, the Lord tells us that at the end of this life, at the end of the personal history of each one, he will give each person "a white stone, with a new name written on the stone which no one knows except the one who receives it" (Rev. 2:17 RF). This "new name" is the person's true identity, hidden now in the risen Jesus.

Whoever is consecrated celibately to the Lord already possesses, in a certain sense, that white stone because in that celibate consecration he or she goes straight to the Jesus who is to come and who marks the end of all history and the end of the personal history of each person—and who holds in his hands the white stone with the secret name.

Consecrated Chastity and the Eucharist

Anthropologist Victor Turner uses the term *liminality* to describe a particular and fundamental quality of sacred rituals—see *Image and Pilgrimage in Christian Culture* (New York: Columbia University Press, 1978), pp. 250-253. In a sacred ritual, whether a Bantu puberty rite or a Moslem prayer or a Catholic Mass, the ritual begins with a separation from the "outside world" and an entering into a special space and time where ordinary social structures (classes, roles) no longer exist, and where therefore a certain equalizing or leveling takes place. Because of this "equalizing" of the participants in the ritual, a phenomenon arises that Turner calls *communitas* (community); *communitas* is a sentiment of oneness and of closeness, of brotherly and sisterly camaraderie, of being equal and united without the usual social structures as barriers. *Communitas* can take place among a group of spectators at a football game or among persons stranded by a strike in an airport; it regularly takes place in religious rituals.

After the ritual, the participants return to their regular social structures. But during the ritual they act in a drama outside social structures, a drama intended to transform them somehow. For example, each Mass is intended to draw us closer to God and to change our lives. A religious ritual is a "rite of passage" from before the ritual to after it, a rite of transition from state A to state B, a "threshold" experience. Hence, a liminal (from the Latin *limen*, "threshold") experience.

The eucharistic sacrifice is liminal; as a religious ritual it has the quality of liminality. Furthermore, it makes present Jesus' final threshold or transition experience, his death and resurrection. And I participate in that Paschal mystery, in the death and resurrection of Jesus, by taking part in the Mass; I move into a liminal "antistructure" situation where I find *communitas.*

In his writings, Victor Turner points out that liminality is found not only in rituals but also in some ways of life. He mentions Benedictine monasticism and early Franciscanism as two examples of liminal ways of life, in which ordinary social roles, classes, and similar structures are dissolved, and where one finds equality and *communitas.* We can extend Turner's examples to embrace all consecrated celibate communities. Consecrated celibate community, then, can be considered liminal, a *limen* or "threshold," a rite of passage to the world to come, a "place" of *communitas.* Ideally, the religious finds both in the Mass and in community what the lay person discovers in many ways but most directly in the Mass: a foretaste of life with God in the world to come. Even if not all religious communities possess real *communitas* always and everywhere, nevertheless most of them did in their initial stages, and still do to some extent.

What makes religious fundamentally "liminal" people is the traditional charisms—poverty, chastity, and obedience. The world seeks control of life and material security, sexual fulfillment, and personal freedom. The charisms of the vows stand as strange, incomprehensible, not corresponding to any worldly norm, value, or category. In his or her consecrated poverty, chastity, and obedience, the religious falls between the structures of society. A religious is neither here nor there, but betwixt and between: in a liminal state, in a transitional and "threshold" state.

Interestingly, both the Eucharist and consecrated celibacy, one as a sacramental sacrifice and the other as a sacrificial vocation, make the future present, stand for the end-time. In the sacrament of the Eucharist, Jesus makes my future present to me in himself. Present for me and holding my future in himself, he makes present my future, which is hidden in him. In this way the Eucharist is an eschatological sacrament, a pledge of future resurrection in Jesus, and the ground of hope. I can hope because, even though I do not know what the future holds, I do know who holds the future—Jesus, who joins me to himself in the Eucharist and, in that communion, stands as the promise that my life will have an ultimately successful outcome in him.

Like the Eucharist, the life of consecrated chastity signifies, witnesses to, Jesus as the Lord and Guarantor of the future, the Father's promise of an ultimately successful outcome for the world and for each of us. Like the Eucharist, consecrated chastity stands for the risen Jesus here and now and for Jesus coming at the end of time, for Jesus already and for Jesus not yet. The life of the consecrated celibate is a life of radical and total hope in Jesus risen, a matter of putting all one's eggs in one basket—into personal relationship with Jesus who is my present hope by being himself my promised future.

Made liminal by my consecrated chastity, identified with the marginal and the oppressed by my poverty and my obedience, I stand with Jesus in the world, but not of it. And I move forward, with him and toward him, in his Spirit, strong with the gifts he gives me and makes grow in me: poverty, obedience, and chastity.

Prayer for the Gift of Chastity

Lord Jesus, I ask you humbly for new grace, for a great increase in the charism of consecrated chastity.

In virtue of your own risen and glorified sexuality, heal me in my own sexuality. Make the rough ways smooth and the crooked ways straight.

Heal me in the whole area of my affectivity, of my capacity to love and to receive love. Teach me your ways, and make me grow in my capacity to love you and to love others, to receive your love and to receive the love of others.

In every holy communion, consecrate my whole self to you by your body, broken on the cross for me and risen for my salvation. Heal me by your five wounds that you still carry for me, and make me whole.

Give me, Lord, your Holy Spirit, and pour out in me your gift of consecrated chastity. Amen.

Chapter Seven

THE THREE PHASES OF RENEWAL

After considering in the four previous chapters the charismatic nature of the religious life, we can return to the subject this book begins with: the evolution of the religious life. Let us look at recent changes, changes that have taken place in almost every order and congregation in the past two decades and that mark the evolution of a religious community during its breakdown period.

Looking at the religious life over the past twenty years, what do we see? Can we outline the changes, sketch the lines of development, and make out—through the fog of details and confusion—some general directions in the recent evolution of the religious life? I would like to try here to draw with large strokes a picture of those changes. My experience is for the most part limited to the Society of Jesus, and therefore my description of change will apply mainly to Jesuit life. But bear with me, see how the shoe fits your own experience, and use my description to help yourself to understand better the changes in your own order or congregation.

Let us look together at the signs of the times, at what has happened and is happening now. Reading the signs of these times in the religious life, we may perhaps understand better the action of the Holy Spirit and where God is taking us.

Renewal of Structures
For one thing, the community structures of the religious life have evolved considerably. In the effort to return to the charisms of the founders and of the first congregation, orders and congregations have simplified their life-styles. Non-monastic apostolic congregations have dismantled excessively monastic structures, retaining only those monastic elements that belong to the authentic charism of the congregation. Monastic orders have recovered the essentials of monasticism. Contemplatives

have simplified the structure of their daily lives, centering everything around their vocation to prayer.

For example, the Jesuits, a strongly non-monastic order, have divested themselves of many monastic practices not in accord with the spirit of St. Ignatius of Loyola—the practice of asking for small permissions, a regular monastic daily order, formation houses in the country away from urban apostolic opportunities, and many other things. Some Jesuits, a diminishing few, have lamented an apparent weakening of discipline and order; but the vast majority intuitively know that the general direction of change in Jesuit community structures has been toward our original Jesuit charism.

Structural evolution has meant different things to different congregations. Apostolic congregations such as the Jesuits have demonasticized greatly; congregations that synthesize the monastic and the non-monastic life-style (e.g., the Passionists) have changed too, but not in the same way as radically non-monastic institutes; monasteries have followed a different path. But all have simplified the everyday structures of the religious life in a return to what they at one time were and to what they are meant to be. This process of structural change remains to some extent incomplete. But the big steps have been taken; the major changes are stabilized. Religious renewal as structural change took place largely between 1962 and 1975. This first phase of the renewal of the religious life is coming to a close. It overlaps with a second phase which began generally in the late 1960s: the phase of *interior* renewal on the part of the individual religious.

Interior Renewal
As the often overly-rigid structures of the religious life became more flexible, we found ourselves freer and therefore more responsible, responsible especially for our spiritual lives. Many of us began to live our vocations in a more interiorized, more prayerful way. Once so many of the exterior props were removed, we began to depend more on the interior life. This second phase of the renewal of the religious life is in full force now. The evidences are numerous: the practically universal

acceptance of daily private prayer as a priority value, the growing emphasis on spiritual direction, the interest in books on the interior life, a more personalized approach to formation, a shift in vocation education methods from exterior witness to stressing interior spiritual values.

The most notable evidence of interior renewal in the religious life is the number of what we can call "second conversions." What is a second conversion? In the Jesuit tradition, the term "second conversion" comes from the writings of the first generations of the Society of Jesus. The decision to give oneself completely to God in the religious life is called the first conversion. The second conversion, according to the Jesuit theory, ordinarily occurs some years after entrance into the postulancy or the novitiate. The theory of the second conversion appears in an institutionalized form in the "tertianship" or "second novitiate," a period of several months of spiritual formation. Many religious orders and congregations plan this for members who have been in the order or congregation for ten or fifteen years. Jesuit tertianships, and as far as I know all tertianships, exist to provide a setting for a second conversion, for a new beginning in the religious life.

The second conversion marks a turning point. It means a new and deeper relationship with the Lord, together with a new zeal and often a new effectiveness in ministry. And it frequently marks the beginning of truly contemplative prayer. The second conversion is, of course, a great grace, something the Lord does, not something we do. We only cooperate.

I find many second conversions taking place today in the religious life. Sometimes they come about within the framework of a person's regular prayer life. After years of fidelity to daily prayer, after times of darkness and dryness, a change takes place—over a period of a few days or a few weeks or a few months. The lights go on. The person is aware that the Lord has moved in and has taken over his or her life, that something new has happened, that what went before served as a preparation for this, that now life begins.

Sometimes the second conversion comes about during a retreat, especially during a directed retreat.

Most of the second conversions I have come across in the religious life, including my own, have come about through the Charismatic Renewal. Commonly, religious men and women who receive the baptism in the Spirit find that it marks a second conversion for them, or the beginning of a second conversion. They have found, in their own words, "a new thirst for prayer," a new love of others and an active concern for their discovering the Lord, a new recollection, faith, joy, peace; "an unimagined freedom that comes from deep inside one"; "a complete renewal and revitalization of my vocation and of my relationships with God."

Community Renewal

At this point we might draw some conclusions:

1. The Lord clearly intends *interior* renewal to go along with the exterior renewal of community structures. And he calls every religious to this interior renewal.

2. If we formulate interior renewal in terms of a "second conversion," we can say that the Lord somehow calls every religious to a second conversion.

3. On the one hand, the Charismatic Renewal's baptism in the Spirit seems to be a privileged means to second conversion for religious. On the other hand, not all religious seem to be attracted to or called to Charismatic Renewal. And that poses a problem: Has the Lord put such a privileged way to a second conversion outside the grasp of many religious, beyond the reach of those not led to Charismatic Renewal?

4. Or does the Lord, who seems not to intend to put all religious into the Charismatic Renewal, intend nevertheless to put some kind of charismatic renewal into all religious?—a renewal of the charisms of poverty, of chastity, of obedience, of the particular congregation, and of the various kinds of ministry and apostolate? If so, then the baptism in the Spirit should somehow be available to every religious, not necessarily in a charismatic prayer group but within the religious life itself.

And why not?

As matters stand, the baptism in the Spirit is most often prayed for in the Charismatic Renewal as a sort of rite of initiation into a prayer group or into a charismatic community. But a religious already has a community.

Practically, it comes to this: Religious who have received the baptism in the Spirit can and should pray over other religious who wish to receive this grace but who do not feel called to go outside the religious life for it. In this way, small groups of religious can form so as to provide a context for those religious who have received the baptism in the Spirit to pray together, to use their gifts in common, and to minister to one another.

The baptism in the Spirit, after all, is not a sacrament, nor even a sacramental. It is the Lord's response to a prayer. The prayer for the "outpouring of the Spirit" or for the "baptism in the Spirit" is simply that: a prayer. And it is a prayer not confined to any special groups or movement.

The prayer for the baptism in the Spirit is a prayer for a new outpouring of the Holy Spirit, for a great outpouring of grace, for a transforming and life-changing grace of interior renewal.

Now that religious are already beginning to pray over their own brothers and sisters for the outpouring of the Holy Spirit, the third phase of the renewal of the religious life has begun. The first phase, the renewal of community structures, has nearly run its course. The second phase, the interior renewal of individual religious, is going full strength. And the third phase, the renewal of community, is beginning. Not only are small groups of religious meeting regularly and praying in the Spirit as well as sometimes praying over other religious for the baptism in the Spirit, but several whole religious houses and convents have received the baptism in the Spirit and live in charismatically renewed local communities.

For it is not only community *structures* that the Lord wants to renew; it is communities themselves. And this, praise him, is what he gives us to look forward to.

I believe we are just beginning a new and great phase of the renewal of the religious life. This new phase coincides in many if not most cases with the later stages of the breakdown period of the order or congregation. Hence, a congregation's breakdown period can become a time of transition to a new founding of the institute. The transition can be made through the renewal of groups within the congregation—not through the renewal of all the institute's members, but through groups that then become the first generation of the new foundation.

Prayer of Self-Offering

Lord Jesus, I offer myself to you to be used for the rebuilding of my religious community. I give myself entirely to you that you may use me as a building block, as a stone in the refoundation, of my community. Make me, Lord, a part of the new temple that you want to build out of and among the ruins of the old one. I feel, Lord, that I may well be a member of the last generation of what my community has been. Let me be a member of the first generation of what, in your providence, it will be.

Most of all, Lord, I offer you myself as an intercessory prayer for my community. Take, Lord, and receive all my freedom, my intelligence, my will, my heart, my whole self. They are yours. Give me only your love and your grace; they are enough for me. And use me as you will for my community—quietly and in the shadows, or actively and taking large steps openly and boldly in faith. As you will, Lord, but use me. I give you myself for the future of my community. Amen.

Chapter Eight

CHARISMATIC RENEWAL
AND RELIGIOUS LIFE

After several years of Catholic Charismatic Renewal, the frontier between the religious life and the Charismatic Renewal remains just that—a frontier, populated by hardy pioneers who try to live their religious vocations in the context of the Renewal, and to live somehow in their religious vocations the new graces and gifts they have received in the Charismatic Renewal. Most of the pioneers struggle in the awareness that:

1. Charismatic Renewal has never known what to do with religious. Many Renewal leaders that I have spoken with feel that the religious life is dying, a moribund life-style, washed up, and that the future lies in charismatic covenant communities such as the Word of God community at Ann Arbor. If the future of the Charismatic Renewal does lie in the covenant communities, what *do* you do with the religious? They already *have* their "covenant communities" in the religious life. Can they serve two masters?

2. Many in the religious life have never known what to do with the Charismatic Renewal. Some major superiors worry because some priests or seminarians or brothers or sisters find their true and real community in charismatic prayer groups. The life and support these religious lack in the local religious community, they find in the local charismatic prayer group—not an ideal situation from anyone's point of view. Religious who do not take part in the Renewal react to those who do, along a spectrum ranging from outright hostility and accusations of heresy to a light banter that veils their uneasiness about matters they do not understand ("How's the Holy Spirit? Ha, ha").

The Charismatic Nature of the Religious Life
The basic problem is clear: Both the religious life and the

Charismatic Renewal are, by their very nature, charismatic. This creates tensions. Religious, called to one type of charismatic community, the religious life, find their charisms renewed outside the religious life in another kind of community, the charismatic prayer group. And so they are torn between two kinds of charismatic community. Other religious, seeing the vitality of Charismatic Renewal groups, feel threatened in various ways and put up emotional defenses against the Renewal.

Yet, when we face this problem, we find that the frontier between the religious life and the Charismatic Renewal teems with possibilities for the renewal of the religious life. It is true also, of course, that the religious life has much to offer to the Charismatic Renewal, but that is beyond the scope of this book.

In the first place, the religious life *is* charismatic in nature. The traditional theological principle maintains that the Church's hierarchical nature finds its institutionalized forms in the pope, in bishops, in parish pastors, and that the Church's charismatic nature finds its institutionalized forms in the various kinds of religious life. This does not, of course, mean that no charisms exist outside the religious life. It does mean that charisms are inherent in the very structure of the religious life.

Furthermore, every individual religious vocation is properly a charism. We can define a charism as a gift from the Lord: (1) that he gives to some persons, but not to all, (2) for service in the building up of the Body of Christ, and (3) as a new way of living in union with him. Not only does a religious vocation fit the definition, but so do the classic three religious vows. Consecrated chastity is a charism ("Each has his own charism"—1 Cor. 7:7). The Franciscan movement of the thirteenth century consisted of a great outpouring of the charism of religious poverty that made it a properly charismatic movement. And religious obedience, as most religious have experienced, is a gift of grace, a charism.

What is more, every religious order and congregation has its own charisms or, rather, its own typical cluster of charisms. Sometimes referred to as "the charism of the founder" or "the charism of the institute," this cluster of charisms marks the style, the spirituality, of a given congregation or order. Often it consists of the charisms given in a particular way to the founder; so, for example, the poverty and joyous simplicity of the Franciscan charism can be seen best in the life of Francis, the Dominican charism in Dominic's own gifts of prayer and evangelization, and the Jesuit charism in the contemplative life and zealous apostolate of Ignatius Loyola. On the other hand, the charism of a given religious group is not a complex of gifts that once existed, but a set of special graces for now; we read the outlines of that charism in the order or congregation today.

Or do we?

Why does the religious life so often look sick or even moribund? Why do so many provinces and even whole congregations clearly appear to be terminal cases? Why do so few men and women enter the religious life today? Why have we lost so many? And where do we find the power of the Lord at work as in the days of Francis and Dominic and Ignatius?

What has gone wrong?

This: Many religious try to live their vocations without calling on the full transforming power of the Holy Spirit. A charismatic vocation absolutely requires the power and the gifts and the charisms of the Holy Spirit. But they are often missing.

I do not want to suggest that the only religious living in the power of the Spirit are those in Charismatic Renewal, nor that the only gifts and charisms of the Spirit are those distinctive of Charismatic Renewal, nor that a religious community must manifest tongues and prophecy to be charismatic.

I *do* mean that the religious life today needs a renewal of the power and the gifts and the charisms of the Spirit.

At the Second Vatican Council, Cardinal Ruffini and a few others found themselves voted down when they claimed that the charisms were only for the early Church, needed then in the infancy of Christianity, but not needed now that we have the institutional Church established. As if to confirm the Council fathers, the Lord began to pour out his gifts in the Catholic Charismatic Renewal only a few years after the Council. Can we say that the charismatic power of the Spirit manifest in the beginnings of our various religious life-styles and spiritualities was only for the beginning?

Or should we pray and hope for a charismatic renewal of the religious life?

And what can we do to further the renewal of the Spirit and of the Spirit's gifts in the religious life, in our own communities? I would like to suggest some practical steps that might be taken, steps that can be adapted to the various local community situations:

1. Religious of the same community or of different communities can get together to (a) pray and use the gifts of the Spirit and (b) share what the Lord is doing in their lives. It is not a question of renewing all religious; some do not even want to be renewed. It is a question of some persons living the religious life in a renewed way, together, in the Spirit, using God's gifts. Men and women religious can meet with others of their community to share and to pray together. How this takes place will depend on the situation. In a community where only a very few have received the outpouring of the Spirit, they could meet informally, perhaps at a regular time daily or bi-weekly, or perhaps frequently but at no fixed time, to share and to pray. Where there are more, a group of up to eight or nine could meet regularly. In some cases, religious from different houses in the same area could perhaps meet weekly for an hour.

In these small pray-share meetings of members of the same community, certain things have been found effective:
• praying over one another for particular needs, special graces or healings or new strength;
• sharing what the *Lord* has done in our lives rather than what we might have done;
• freely using the gifts, especially tongues, prophecy, and Scripture in prayer.

Naturally, any isolation from the rest of the community is to be avoided. On the contrary, religious who have not experienced the renewal of the charisms of the religious life may want to participate in the small informal meeting of their brothers or sisters. Together they can pray for the outpouring of the Spirit, especially for an increase of the charism of that particular congregation and for an increase in any particular charisms which seem appropriate (teaching, leadership, service, music, and so on).

These small groups, meeting on a regular basis, could intercede for the local community, the province, and the whole congregation. They can be a means of bringing charismatic renewal into religious community.

Men and women religious are doing this *now.* I know personally of several such small groups in Ireland, Italy, England, Scotland, and the United States. I belong to one.

It works.

2. Regional and national meetings of religious of the same order or congregation who in some way participate in Charismatic Renewal have proven successful. The American Jesuits in the Renewal, for example, meet every August for a few days. This holds also for men and women religious who share the same spirituality; for example, there is a regular charismatic meeting in western Ireland of Dominican men and women.

3. Local charismatic meetings can be held every month or every few months for all men and women religious in the area. Where this has been done, the Lord has moved in great power. Here in Rome, over the past few years, we have had some retreat days for priests and others for sisters; but the days of greatest grace have been the retreat days for all religious: priests, brothers, and sisters.

Charismatic Renewal in Religious Life

Reading the Charismatic Renewal as a sign of the times, and called to a life of conversion and of living out the charisms of our call, we can ask the Lord to do *for us, in* our congregations and orders, what he does in charismatic prayer groups all over the world. The idea is *not* to get religious into existing charismatic covenant communities, nor even into the multitudinous charismatic prayer groups, but to look to the Lord for renewal of the religious life through second conversions and greater charismatic graces *in* the religious life.

Does the Lord call us all into the Charismatic Renewal? No.

Does the Lord call us all to charismatic renewal within our communities? Certainly yes.

The Lord has already begun to renew charismatically the religious life. The golden age of the religious life is not in the past, when we had more vocations, more structural support from the system, more exterior conformity to the law. The golden age of the religious life is in the future that we look to in faith, "the assurance of things hoped for, the conviction of things unseen" (Heb. 11:1 RSV). That future has already begun, and we are in it.

In the present time, in this time of dwindling numbers in the religious life, the Lord astonishes us by pouring out great and powerful charisms of witnessing, of preaching, of serving, of teaching, of leading; graces of poverty, chastity, obedience; graces of contemplative prayer; graces of zeal and courage and martyrdom. The Holy Spirit, the Spirit of the last times, the eschatological Spirit, comes into the religious life now in power to those who look to the Lord for renewal.

Is this a kind of vision of the future, a prophetic view? No. It is happening now. We can open our eyes and see it; and we can read the signs.

Most of us stand amid the ruins of the breakdown phase of our order or congregation. But we can see, amid the ruins themselves, the Lord beginning to lay a new foundation.

Prayer for Guidance

Unless you build the house, Lord, we build in vain. Guide me along the paths that you want me to take. Teach me your way for me. Lead me to the persons you want me to share with and to pray with, and lead me to share with them and to pray with them the way you want me to.

Give me, Jesus, a new outpouring of your Holy Spirit, of all the charisms of my religious life, and of all the gifts of the Spirit that you want me to have. Let me walk in your Spirit in love and in power.

Spirit of Jesus, Holy Spirit, Spirit of the living God, fall afresh on me. Melt me, mold me, fill me, use me. Amen.

Experiences

INTRODUCTORY NOTE

The following experiences describe what can happen when the innately charismatic nature of the religious life is given its proper emphasis. In these experiences, an appropriate emphasis on the charismatic elements of religious life was achieved by adapting what has been learned from the Charismatic Renewal movement to that other charismatic movement that is the religious life.

Father Francesco Caniato, S.J., organized the first three annual eight-day Jesuit retreats given in Italy in a way that brought out the emphasis on charisms that Ignatius Loyola made clear in his *Spiritual Exercises*. In Experience One, Father Caniato describes the second and third such retreats. Four other such retreats have been given to Jesuits in North America: one in 1980, two in 1981, and one in 1982; several others are planned. The first such retreat in Great Britain took place in late July 1982; there was a similar retreat, open to all religious men and women in Great Britain, in early August 1982, and more are planned.

The basis of Jesuit spirituality is the *Spiritual Exercises* of St. Ignatius Loyola; every Jesuit spends at least eight days every year following the Exercises. Those of us Jesuits who have participated in retreats such as those Father Caniato describes know how the Lord works powerfully in them to renew us in our Jesuit vocation.

In Experience Two, Sister Anne Field, O.S.B., tells of the charismatic prayer group at Stanbrooke Abbey. Elsewhere there are contemplative convents in which has emerged an appropriate charismatic pattern that involves all the members of the community. In such convents, there is no need for a prayer group; the whole monastery lives continuously in the Spirit; charismatic gifts are used regularly in the Mass and in the Divine Office. Sister Anne's situation, however, is more typical, and so her account of it may help many who find themselves in similar circumstances.

Experience One

JESUIT RETREATS IN ITALY

by Francesco Caniato, S. J.

August 1979

At Villa Cavalletti, near Grottaferrata and not far from Rome, a group of Jesuit Fathers and Brothers made the Exercises in the spirit of the Renewal in the Spirit. Fathers Tommaso Beck and Francis Sullivan gave the points for meditation and the instructional talks.

The daily schedule was: 8:00 A.M., lauds; 9:15 A.M., points for meditation; 4:00 P.M., instruction; 6:15 P.M., eucharistic celebration; 9:00 P.M., prayer in small groups.

Lauds were recited and prayed before the exposed Blessed Sacrament, with time left between psalms for spontaneous vocal prayer.

The points for meditation, like the afternoon instruction conference, were preceded and followed by hymns and spontaneous prayers of witnessing and praise, which exemplified in a group way the traditional Ignatian preludes of the presence of the Lord and the *id quod volo*, and the colloquies.

Father Beck presided at the eucharistic concelebrations, giving an extension and a completion, in the evening Eucharist, to his meditation thoughts of the morning.

The prayer in smaller groups gave each individual an opportunity to express himself better: in spontaneous prayer and in requests for prayer for himself and over himself, and in sharing his spiritual desolations and consolations. Here our friendly communication, our knowledge of one another, our mutual esteem and love, and our conversion also grew, as will be made clear further on.

After supper, Fathers Beck and Sullivan met with another priest to go over the day's progress and to prepare the following day's schedule.

At the end of the eighth day, all the retreatants made a general review of the experience.

We would like to report on certain features of this spiritual experience, which was the second such venture, the first having taken place in September 1978.

In St. Ignatius' Exercises, the retreatant seeks God's will for him. He disposes himself as well as he can for that purpose, so that "the Creator and Lord in person may communicate himself to the devout soul in quest of the divine will, embrace it with his love and glory, and dispose it for the way in which it can better serve God in the future" (Annotation 15).

What is this communication of himself, this embrace of the soul by God's love and glory, if not a new mission of the Holy Spirit, with his gifts of grace? For that reason, in our experience of the Ignatian Exercises we kept our constant attention focused on both the Holy Spirit and Annotation 15.

Praise and the "Principle and Foundation"

As a result of our persevering and living openness to the Holy Spirit, we experienced in ourselves during this retreat, in a more powerful way, the Lord's communication of himself and his embrace of our souls, of which Annotation 15 speaks. In particular, the Holy Spirit gave himself to us in the praise called for by the Principle and Foundation.

A praise that was not only theoretical, but that we expressed, over and over, in our individual and group praying. A praise that arose from our realization of the Lord's increasing mercy despite our sinning, disorder, and powerlessness. A praise that we gave to the Lord of our lives, which, flowing from the Principle and Foundation, expressed it again and again in every prelude, meditation, and point of our Exercises. For we knew that in each Ignatian meditation and contemplation the soul must let itself be quickened and renewed by the Principle and Foundation, must express the Principle and Foundation by praising and exalting the Lord above itself and above all things, seeking to serve him in the fullest possible way.

It was a praise that we voiced with joyous singing, even in tongues, and with the spontaneous gesture of our bodies, in whatever way our hearts suggested.

Seeing the Disorder in Our Lives

We felt, as a fruit of the Holy Spirit's inner communication, a profound awareness of our sins, a sense of the disorder of our actions, and that knowledge of the world which we asked for in the Triple Colloquy of the First Week. That realization was a communication from the Spirit and his loving embrace.

This knowledge was not a morbid digging into the past, but rather something that each of us felt drawn to do, so that we confessed to our brothers, with spontaneity, sincerity, and ease, the disorder and sin in our lives, in the sacrament of reconciliation or one of the other gatherings, e.g., the penitential service before the liturgy or the small prayer groups.

The Grace of Amendment and Healing

The Holy Spirit's gift of a knowledge of our inner evil brought us to ask him, as St. Ignatius suggests (EE. 63), for the grace of "amendment" or healing of the heart.

We prayed at length for our inner healing, both together in one large group and in small groups. In the groups each one asked his companions to pray for him and over him, as St. James recommends (5:16 JB): "So confess your sins to one another, and pray for one another, and this will cure you."

During this brotherly praying for one another we felt the healing presence of the Lord, the loving embrace of his Spirit. Indeed, the Lord's healing presence is a social fact, just as our sin is.

Conversion

St. Ignatius' Exercises tend to dispose us and renew us for a second conversion. This consists in our total submission to God's action, in our "disappropriation" of ourselves as we shift the axis of our lives, making God the center, the measure, and the goal of our thoughts and actions.

All this adds up to a recognition that we are sinful creatures to whom God has given life—and the promise of salvation. The second conversion means, therefore, living the Principle and Foundation.

This is a work of God from within us, a healing in depth, a liberation: The Spirit himself enables us to accept ourselves. That is his gift, which we can receive from him only if we abandon ourselves to him.

For us, this change was brought about from outside us: by the witness of our brothers, especially their praise, through which we could see and feel something of the very action of the Spirit, his loving embrace.

Evidence of our progressive conversion was our growing ease in expressing ourselves and communicating with one another, especially by confessing openly that we are sinners.

The Charism of the Society of Jesus
In the Second Week, Ignatius has us ask for one grace after another: not to be deaf to the Lord's call, but to offer ourselves to him, helped by his warmth and energy, to know him more intimately, and to follow him so as to be received under his banner in poverty and humiliation.

Evidently, all that is not our doing, but a letting ourselves be conquered by the Lord through the power of his Spirit. And that is precisely what we felt. We praised the Lord for the long succession of graces that we have received since our entrance into the Society and that make up, with their culmination in the Third Degree of Humility, the very charism of the Jesuit.

But we felt strongly that we should renew those graces, as St. Paul urged in his second letter to Timothy (1:5-7 JB): "I am reminded of the sincere faith that you have; it came to life first in your grandmother Lois, and your mother Eunice, and I have no doubt that it is the same faith in you as well. That is why I am reminding you now to fan into a flame the gift that God gave you when I laid my hands on you. God's gift was not a spirit of timidity, but the Spirit of power, and love, and self-control."

With greater intensity in this Second Week we raised up our voices in praise for this charism of our vocation. With greater availability and humility we opened ourselves to the Holy

Spirit, as Mary and the apostles did when they were persevering in the Cenacle and were of one mind in prayer (Acts 1:12-14).

We prayed over one another according to the Lord's invitation: "Ask and it will be given to you; search and you will find; knock, and the door will be opened to you. . . . The heavenly Father will give the Holy Spirit to those who ask him!" (Lk. 11:9-13 JB). We prayed for a new mission or outpouring of the Holy Spirit with his gifts, first of all for the gifts that are proper to the Jesuit vocation, that we already received—but that we may have buried like the talents in the gospel parable (Mt. 25:14-30).

And so we sang as if we truly meant it the *Veni Creator Spiritus* that Father General invoked at the end of the Procurators Congregation recently: "Lord, I need your Spirit, that divine force that has transformed so many human personalities, making them capable of extraordinary deeds and extraordinary lives. . . . Not only did they become capable of tremendous acts of boldness and strength, but they took on new personalities and felt themselves able to perform difficult missions. . . . Feeling the difficulty of my mission, I desire your profound action in my soul, not only that you descend, but that 'you repose in me' and give me those wondrous gifts that you lavish on your elect. . . . These gifts will open up for the Society an era of happiness and holiness."

In this way we felt the force of the Heart of Jesus, which poured out on us the Holy Spirit, and we rediscovered the importance of this devotion that is distinctive of our Society. Especially here, in the heart of the Exercises, we felt ourselves embraced by the love of the Heart of Jesus.

We conclude these notes with a list of the witness that various of our number gave at the end of the Exercises:
• I felt all of Ignatius' ideas and emphases with exceptional intensity.
• We came to know one another profoundly, and that knowledge was further strengthened by our exchange of pardon and our ready communication.
• We joyously felt anew our Jesuit vocation.

- There was a strong involvement and motion of soul in all of us.
- I had an experience of the *Societas amoris.*
- I felt embraced by the Lord.
- Our praying over one another and for one another did me so much good.
- We loved one another deeply: We felt that we were Church.
- We were renewed as a Society of Jesus and as Church because the Lord was put back as the center of our lives, thanks to the Holy Spirit.
- I felt sincerely and fraternally welcomed by everyone present.
- I was surprised to find myself weeping with consolation.
- We felt powerful consolations and desolations.
- I was keenly aware that everything is a gift of the Holy Spirit, especially the Third Degree of Humility.

September 1979
At Galloro outside Rome, another group of Jesuits did a course of the Spiritual Exercises which, like the preceding one at Villa Cavalletti, was quickened by the force of the Renewal in the Spirit.

There were thirty-two Jesuits in this second group—fathers, brothers, a scholastic, and a novice—all but a bare handful from the Province of Italy. During the eight days, several visitors came to spend the day praying with us: Fathers Domenico Grasso, Luis González, and Carlo M. Martini.

The daily schedule and the presentation of the Exercises were quite similar to what we had known in the previous retreat at Villa Cavalletti. Fathers Tommaso Beck and Robert Faricy gave the points for meditation.

There were four smaller prayer groups, whose leaders met peridically with Fathers Beck and Faricy to decide on any changes or new programing for the retreat.

Here we will single out a few of the aspects that came out with particular force during the eight days.

Our Group Prayer as an Announcement
Before one of our directors would give points, we regularly had

a period of prayer in common with him, as in the retreat at Villa Cavalletti. It was spontaneous prayer under the motion of the Spirit, as recommended by St. Paul ("We . . . worship in accordance with the Spirit of God"—Phil. 3:3 JB).

That sort of prayer often became a true announcing of the word of the Lord, in which each one would read, with the spontaneity of the Spirit, verses from the Scriptures that formed, even in advance, the topic that the director would give as matter for meditation.

In this way, our little praying community became prophetic and evangelizing. The group prayer became an announcement. The director's role was in that sense anticipated, limited, guided, applied, reinforced, and integrated by the community in prayer.

We tried to do what Paul recommended to the communities at Colossae and Corinth: "Let the message of Christ, in all its richness, find a home with you. Teach each other, and advise each other, in all wisdom. With gratitude in your hearts sing psalms and hymns and inspired songs to God" (Col. 3:16 JB); "You must want love more than everything else; but still hope for the spiritual gifts as well, especially prophecy. . . . You can all prophesy in turn, so that everybody will learn something and everybody will be encouraged" (1 Cor. 14:1 and 31 JB).

Turning to Mary
Whenever Mary became present among us through our living faith in her, our group prayer of announcement became more vigorous. Thus we understood why the apostles and disciples in the Cenacle had Mary with them, as they persevered and were at one there in prayer (see Acts 1:14).

Mary helped us with force and sweetness to hear the call of her Son, our King and Lord, and later to contemplate the mysteries of his life. We also rediscovered the simple beauty of her rosary.

Contemplating the Mysteries of the Lord
More than two-thirds of the thirty-day Exercises consists of a simple contemplation of the Lord in the mysteries of his birth, life, death, and resurrection. And the month ends with a

contemplation—the Contemplation for Obtaining Love.

It is clear, then, that among the various "manners of praying" according to our spirituality, Ignatius proposes contemplation as the main one, so that we will be touched, conquered, and renewed in the Lord, through his Spirit (see Eph. 4:20-24; Phil. 3:7-11). And so in our Exercises we offered the Eucharist one day in order that the gift of contemplation proper to our vocation would be renewed in us, and within the limits of a retreat of eight days like ours we spent most of the Second, Third, and Fourth Weeks contemplating the Lord.

Together we began the contemplations of the Lord's mysteries, just as together we had announced the matter for the meditations. Then we would read an excerpt from the gospel; after that, each would pray, repeating aloud this or that word or phrase. Thus we let the Lord's own word echo and be revealed in us, avoiding suffocating it by our reasonings. We listened to it, welcomed it, adored it, as the brothers repeated it, leaving a space for silent contemplation between one announcement and the next.

With amazement we noticed how alive the word of the Lord is, laden with the presence of the Word in person, the Lord. We contemplated the Lord alive in our midst, who by his presence gave greater light and strength to his written word that we were proclaiming.

We discovered the majesty of the Scriptures that bear the Lord within them, like the bread of the Eucharist. A living Bread it was, just as he is the living Word (see Heb. 4:12). We were attentive not to let fall a single fragment of this holy word.

We then continued individually our contemplation that we had begun together. Many of us felt the need to contemplate the mystery of the Lord's passion and death for a whole night, each of us adoring for an hour his memorial, the Eucharist. Indeed, some watched that way all night long.

Some Testimonies
At the end of this retreat we gathered the witness of the participants, some of which repeated those given at the end of the previous retreat, while others brought out new thoughts:

- All of us were unified, made as one in the Spirit, so that we were able to give and receive: Each of us was a sacrament of the Lord for his brother. In our brotherly communication, we felt the Lord passing through us. The gifts of each one were placed at the disposal of all the rest.
- We were all little and equal during the prayer in common. All were disciples, all were masters.
- I felt pain every time I moved my arm. The doctors had found a spur in my elbow-joint. During the First Week, I asked the Lord to heal me as a sign of the inner healing that he was performing in our hearts. I felt myself healed. Now the pain is completely gone.
- Each day the Lord gave us a new charism: poverty, humility, fraternal charity, union of souls. The Exercises done this way will always be fresh and new.
- I discovered the sense of prayer and the power of the Scriptures.
- I was seriously ill—in the sense that I wasn't praying any more. Here, I immediately found a substantial help for prayer, the charism of prayer. The first three days I had just let myself drag along. For me, the First Week lasted four days; at the end I seized the occasion of our small prayer group's meeting to make a public confession, since I was finally on the way to an inner healing.
- I learned what "lived" prayer and the "prayed" word of God are.
- I learned to proclaim that Jesus is Lord. Confessing him Lord of our life, we will achieve union of souls.
- I feel interiorly healed. I no longer hold grudges against anyone.

Experience Two

BENEDICTINE LIFE AT STANBROOKE ABBEY

by Sister Anne Field, O.S.B.

It is ten years now since our community began to be involved in Charismatic Renewal and seven years since the release of the Spirit among us became contagious and irrepressible. I shall not describe the experience that has been the subject of innumerable testimonies throughout the world, since it is fundamentally the same for all. In an enclosed community, however, the style of our involvement is necessarily different from that of large lay groups, and it might be worth looking at what the Lord has done for us in a Benedictine monastery, together with some of the problems we have encountered.

Because, as Scripture says, the Spirit of God is both unique and manifold (Wis. 7:22), the variety of gifts with which God endows us will not pull us in opposite directions. God's gift to a monastic community will above all be to deepen its commitment to its own vocation and to throw new light on the essentially charismatic nature of monasticism. The search for God in prayer and Scripture, serving God in work and worship, listening to God's word addressed to us daily, repentance, conversion, the common life, the humble service of the community, faith in the transforming work of the Spirit in our lives—all these aspects of the Rule of Benedict play a great part in what the Spirit is saying to the churches through the Renewal and through charismatic communities everywhere. What is *new* for us is the desire and readiness to share what the Lord is saying to us, to expect God's power to be at work among us, to pray together spontaneously, to seek God's word for us as a community, to communicate on a level that used to be regarded as one's own private relationship with the Lord.

Without going into the question of whether the monastic and the contemplative life are identical, I should like to touch upon one or two difficulties encountered by contemplatives in regard to the Renewal. Some people are uneasy about the Charismatic Renewal because it seems to be throwing overboard the treasures of the ascetical and mystical tradition of the Church. They do not see how all this spontaneous praying and claiming and rejoicing fits in with the teaching of the great saints who have mapped out the ways of contemplative prayer. Charismatic Renewal looks too much like sanctity in three easy lessons. These people have learned from the classical writings on prayer to have a great distrust of sensible devotion and consolations on account of the dangers of delusion and of seeking the gifts rather than the Giver. They feel that the dark night is by far the safer course to follow. They look forward to union with God in heaven; they believe they are united with God already by grace, but they neither expect nor even desire any experience of this now. They are used to waiting patiently, stoically enduring, not really expecting anything to happen.

One of the things that lies behind this uneasiness is that our classical training in spirituality has inhibited us from thinking we can have any experience of God until we have attained a high state of prayer. We tend to regard any vivid awareness of God's presence and of the inspirations of the Holy Spirit as characteristic of the unitive way, whereas the majority of religious who suppose themselves to be either in the purgative or illuminative way expect to have to slog along, *trying* to improve in the practice of the presence of God, *trying* to follow the leadings of the Spirit, but finding God's action hindered most of the time by their own psychological processes. Since, according to the scholastic axiom, whatever is received is received according to the disposition of the recipient, a person who believes he or she must spend a long time in the lower states before attaining to unitive prayer can effectively block the perception of God's presence. Often people are inhibited by the notion that it is God's will that they should spend their whole life in an arid desert. (This is far from the climate of the New Testament.)

This is not to say that such people love God less, are less spiritual or dedicated or prayerful than charismatics; they may well be ahead of them in self-denial, patient endurance, and generous service. The one thing they seem to lack is that act of surrender, that yielding in confident expectation that God will fulfill divine promises, promises that are for the claiming here and now. They can be like St. Peter, whose reaction to God's invitation to take and eat was, "Certainly not, Lord! I have never eaten anything unclean." Contemplatives can react to the idea of being baptized in the Spirit with, "Certainly not, Lord—I have never sought consolations."

There is a certain confusion over the notion of consolations, similar to the confusion of *experience* with *emotion*. The fact is that experience is related to faith, emotion to feelings. We all know the testimonies of people whose experience of the release of the Spirit was highly emotional, and of those who felt nothing at all though they knew afterwards that there had been a real change in their lives. Both were *experiences*; after all, one can experience God's absence, a state hardly to be called emotional. Faith can well overflow into feelings, but faith comes first.

Baptism in the Spirit does not at all eliminate the dark ways of faith from our lives, nor is it a shortcut to sanctity. Those who are overwhelmed with awareness of God's presence frequently undergo a desert experience afterwards and have to learn how to walk in bare faith. But there is a different quality to that faith; it now has an expectancy and a trust that God's power is available and active here and now.

Another reason for doubts concerning the involvement of contemplatives in the Renewal is that those who have advanced along the paths of contemplative prayer have learned with ever-increasing certainty that God is beyond all concepts and images; prayer becomes more and more stripped and bare, consisting of naked faith, unfelt love, an almost imperceptible thread of hope, the will's clinging to God. What place is there in contemplative houses for prayer meetings with their simple enthusiasm, choruses, testimonies, tongues, and verbalized prayers? These may be all very well for laypeople who are new to prayer, we hear, but they are not necessary on the higher slopes of Mount Carmel. In fact they can be dangerous.

Here we have a common mistake: the equating of the Charismatic Renewal with a certain style of prayer meetings. In my own community there are nuns who are fully committed to the Renewal but who after a time have decided that the prayer meetings are not for them. Such decisions are respected; we know these nuns are praying with us, often at the same time, and we are united with them. At the same time there is a regret, because at the prayer meeting the Holy Spirit is able to speak to us through the gifts of teaching, wisdom, knowledge, and prophecy, that he leads us as a body, and that we grow together in that horizontal relationship which has often been neglected in contemplative communities. Those in the prayer groups can, however, make the mistake of trying to imitate the more exuberant style of large prayer meetings elsewhere, and of feeling there is something wrong with them if they do not have loud praise and the other ingredients of big gatherings. As Abbot David Parry remarks in *Not Mad, Most Noble Festus,* "contemplative nuns will work out for themselves a very different prayer from that encountered at popular parish level." But by praying together, supporting one another and ministering to one another, we build up one another and encourage one another to be faithful to that naked clinging of the will to God to which we are called; and one of the gifts the Spirit gives to every member of a contemplative group is an increased hunger and thirst for God in the depths of our hearts where he calls to us in ways beyond concepts and words. Just as it is traditionally recognized that liturgical prayer feeds our individual prayer and that such prayer helps our participation in the liturgy, so both enrich our shared prayer, and the Renewal brings new dimensions to them both.

This brings me to another problem encountered perhaps especially by Benedictines. There is in the monastic tradition the noble heritage of liturgical prayer, beauty in worship, dignified rendering of the Divine Office, the offering to God of the best the human spirit can bring in the sphere of music, language, and reverent ceremonial. Are not the choruses and jargon of the Renewal unworthy of this ideal?

The Renewal cannot be identified with guitars and pop music. Persons steeped in church music may indeed find these a stumbling block. There is no reason why a monastic group should not sing the kind of songs that suits them best. However, monastic life is not to be identified with either plainchant or solemn liturgy, and it sometimes happens that God asks us to humble ourselves and become like little children. One nun in our group found the choruses an insurmountable obstacle until she discovered that the breakthrough to the release of the Spirit came only when she was able to surrender and join in the singing. To witness her joy on that occasion was a great experience for the rest of us. Still, each group should be able to develop "wrappings" for the "jewel" that conform to its members' needs. We should have enough confidence in God's particular love and affirmation of us to know that by being ourselves we can receive his gifts. Singing in tongues often has a quality of great beauty; on the other hand, there may well be a greater place for shared silence in a monastic prayer meeting.

There is, however, a danger of being too self-conscious about being contemplatives at a prayer meeting. If we rule out the more popular elements by insisting on too much silence, we shall indeed get it, but it will be a dead and isolating kind of silence. "In a life of silence," a Cistercian monk said once, "there is no need to provide oases of silence." Our need is more often to break through barriers of noncommunication in our communities so that we can be really open to one another, and so that the Spirit can speak to us through one another.

Enclosed nuns may sometimes feel a pang of envy when they hear reports of Spirit-filled charismatic conferences, mass prayer meetings, healing services, and gifted leaders. Sometimes we do have the stimulus of praying with other groups who come to us. But the possibility of national and regional meetings is ruled out for us. All the more reason to trust in the Lord's willingness to give us every gift we need where we are, and to realize that there are many more charismatic gifts than those ordinarily listed.

A real difficulty in our life is to find a stretch of time for a prayer meeting when all can be present. Three quarters of an hour a week is the most we can manage here. Obviously this does not allow for some of the elements in parish groups; but we have the great advantage of being nourished continually by the word of God at our daily liturgy and in our *lectio divina*, so that there is not the need for scripture readings and doctrinal teaching. Teachings tend to arise out of the texts of the liturgy. The Lord frequently "anoints" a word for us, and we are amazed at the riches of sharing this brings. Another difficulty is that of not disturbing others in the community who are not members of the group. It is amazingly hard to find a place where you can sing without distracting somebody else! This is an added reason why our prayer meetings tend to be fairly quiet. But the Renewal goes far beyond the weekly prayer meetings; it is the willingness to share, the openness to one another during the day, the learning to forgive and be forgiven, the small sessions for physical or inner healings, the growth in discernment, the joy in witnessing to the good news to visitors, the support we give to the rest of the community by praying with people who come to us in need of help, the experience of what it means to step out and act in the faith that what we have prayed for we have already received. All this and much more the Spirit is giving us; not that it is something special to the monastic life or on the other hand something different from it, for the monastic life is simply a life *per ducatum evangelii,* the Christian life proclaimed not by preaching in the marketplace but by being lived in community.

There are many signs that the Charismatic Renewal as a whole is at a point of new growth. We are conscious of this in our community. May the Holy Spirit lead us all into greater maturity and empower us for whatever is to come!